SOCIETY, SCIENTISTS AND THE SPIRIT

Ranan Banerji, Ph.D.

Bloomington, IN   Milton Keynes, UK

authorHOUSE™

AuthorHouse™
1663 Liberty Drive, Suite 200
Bloomington, IN 47403
www.authorhouse.com
Phone: 1-800-839-8640

AuthorHouse™ *UK Ltd.*
500 Avebury Boulevard
Central Milton Keynes, MK9 2BE
www.authorhouse.co.uk
Phone: 08001974150

First published by AuthorHouse 6/6/2006

ISBN: 1-4259-3112-X (sc)

Library of Congress Control Number: 2006903512

Printed in the United States of America
Bloomington, Indiana

This book is printed on acid-free paper.

To Lekha, my fellow experimenter

TABLE OF CONTENTS

Preface

This is a book written by a scientist, with the hope that some scientists will find it worth reading, and read it with an open scientific mind.

As a scientist, I have seen no contradiction between scientific study and spiritual exercises. While studying the properties of matter as a Physicist, I had no difficulty in telling myself that I was studying one aspect of the Divine phenomenon. But, again as a scientist, I found it somewhat unsatisfactory that the link between the two aspects of what I called the Divine phenomenon was very tenuous. Dualism was never satisfactory to me.

The spiritual underpinnings of my exercises has never been tied to any specific religious dogma. I have talked to and learned from leaders of the Ramakrishna Vivekananda Society as well as many close associates in the Religious Society of Friends as well as the Jesuit community. Some of the disciples of Swami Chinmayananda also helped me deepen my understanding of the Vedantic meditational practices.

My ideas started congealing quite rapidly after I became aware of the book, "The Self-Aware Universe" by my old friend Amit Goswami, Professor Emeritus of Physics at the University of Oregon. I found in it an approach to spirituality in excellent consonance with what I was looking for, since it linked the concept of the Spirit with Physics in a seamless way.

From then on the thoughts I have expressed in this book started developing. I was helped very much by interaction with many individuals and in the course of many different projects and efforts. I received help and encouragement from Dr. Tom Weissert, Secretary of the Society for the Study of Time. I also had many discussions with Amit Goswami. During a time when I was lecturing on these matters at the Technical University of Vienna, Dr. Werner Schimanovich and Dr. Georg Gottlob introduced me to the concept of Morphogenetic Fields developed by Rupert Sheldrake. I began to see clear theoretical relationships between his ideas and Goswami's. This happened inspite of some efforts by some friends to keep me from connecting the two.

I do not quite know when I began to see relationships between what I was writing and the social malaise so ably described by Michael Lerner in "The Politics of Meaning". But there also my understanding of the Vedantic practices were of great help. I am indebted to my son-in-law, Joshua Spielberg, for acquainting me with Rabbi Lerner's work.

After that the exact presentation of the thoughts in this book went through many revisions, aided by "the school of hard knocks". During this period, I was helped in my presentation by my dear daughter, Anindita Spielberg and my friend William Patterson of the Haddonfield meeting of friends.

The first draft of the approximate form of this book did not get completed till about 2001. All subsequent rewrites occurred under the very able tutelage of my friend Susanna Dodgson of the Haddonfield Friends Meeting. I owe a deep debt of gratitude to her for the continuous guidance I received from her about the proper presentation of my ideas. I also owe a debt of gratitude to my relative, Dev Kar of the International Monetary Fund, for clarifying some ideas about economics.

I am indebted to all of these sources

CHAPTER 1
Introduction: Society and Science

This book is written to be understandable and accessible to the general reading public. Nevertheless, I would like to describe the book as a message and a request for the scientific community. In the last few hundred years, scientists have led and molded both society and social thought. The general public has known science through technology – the many amenities of life and of comfort that scientific thinking has allowed man to produce and sell. And in this role, scientists hold a special place of respect and leadership in society. But some scientists also know themselves as thinkers, dedicated to the discovery of truth. Because of the respect in which scientists are held, scientific truth has shaped social thinking also. I feel that because of this special role scientists play in society, they bear some responsibility for social welfare. My own belief is that they need to make some changes in their belief system so that they can lead society away from some harmful directions and lead it into a beneficial path.

I myself am a scientist by training and by inclination. By that I do not mean that I am just conversant with scientific techniques and their applications. My approach to all problems, rather, is scientific. In everything I study I try to descend to the logical basis of what I am studying. It is my scientific credentials in Physics, Mathematics, Computer Science and Logic that gives me confidence that I can speak of Science and its Philosophical underpinnings with some authority.

As I said above, I am going to argue for a significant paradigm shift in Science. I intend to make the point that this shift would do no harm to the body of science and to scientific practices of the present. On the other hand, it would open science to new horizons and remove some significant existing anomalies and confusions. I shall suggest adding an extra axiom (scientists often call these "laws") to the presently accepted axioms of Physics.

As I have said above, there is another equally important point I intend to make. I feel that if this new paradigm is accepted and asserted by scientists, it would be of great social benefit. It would lead to a much more inclusive and benign society. In the rest of this book I shall try to establish these two points.

It behooves me as a scientist to set out what I mean when I say "Society", "Science" and "the Spirit" in the title of this book, at least roughly. By "Society" I shall mean mostly the social condition in the United States. But I have to point out also that this condition has influenced the condition in many parts of the world. This influence has weakened many aspects of other societies, some good, some harmful. It has also strengthened many other pernicious aspects of those societies. So when I say "Society" I will often also mean human society in general.

My definition of "Science" can for the present be taken to be the usual technical definition of the term. But just as I have done above for "Society", I shall have to sharpen that definition as I proceed with the book. However, I will not feel compelled to adhere to every fixation that the scientific community may have.

The word "Spirit" I would like to leave fuzzy for the present. The definition can only get sharpened through a lot of discussion. Without those discussions we shall run the risk of getting mired in many contradictory conceptions associated with that word. But no other single word is available to the English language to describe what I am going to describe. Unfortunately, some of the concepts associated with the term "Spiritual" is deeply disturbing to me and to many other thinking people. On the other hand, many other connotations associated with the word coincides well with what I shall try to develop as we go.

While I am appreciative of the many good things about the American culture, I also feel that we are in a social mess. Many people we read about and know about seem to have lost their feeling of social responsibility. There are many people, of course, who have continued with the old ideals of community and shared responsibility; but there are also a large number of people whose behavior, like "road rage", does not reflect those ideals in the least. Our attitude towards consumption does not reflect responsibility. No society can remain stable unless it is based on a universally shared set of responsibilities. So signs of unrest are everywhere.

Michael Lerner[1] has concluded on the basis of many research results, that modern society is suffering from great malaise. People, even in the middle of plenty, do not feel secure about their future and the future of their children. They feel isolated from their neighbors. Neighborliness as a concept does not hold, either in affluent suburbia or in the poorest slums. Employees can not rely on their employers to protect their interests. Employers do not feel safe in assuming that their employees will have the interests of the employers at heart. Society has become a gigantic network of people striving for their own narrow interest at the expense of everyone else. In the process, all our interests are in jeopardy. This includes even the true interests of the most powerful and the richest.

And yet, Lerner's research finds that people are deeply dissatisfied by this state of affairs. But they do not know what to do about them. As a result they fall prey to the simplistic theories advanced by the extreme right and the extreme left. And once more they serve as fodders to the self-centered power-play of the special interests.

Lerner feels that this is because ours has become a godless society. Yet many people who consider themselves to be religious, set extreme examples of hatred, greed and destructiveness. The very concept of God becomes suspect because of this. Thinking people, in their search for an acceptable alternative to religion, have turned to science to form the basis of a good society. And if goodness consisted only of the availability of comfort and enjoyment, then science (actually technology) certainly appears to have fulfilled the promise in some places. But the malaise continues.

Many people will agree with me that the troubles of our society is of a cultural nature. The dictum "Nice people do not win ball games" has become a part of our culture. Nobody seems to know how to avoid these. Those who feel they know, and with whom I may even agree, rely heavily on Government action. To me, any form of coercion - even by an elected government - indicates a lack of community consciousness, which itself is contrary to social responsibility. Social debate is often replaced by strident altercation.

I shall argue that these troubles arise because the present culture of the western world is based on what the scientists believe about the nature of things. Most scientists believe that the central entity of the universe is matter. It would not be so harmful if this belief permeated only the physical sciences; the study of matter can continue the way it has without any immediate path correction. Unfortunately, this belief in materialism has also become the basis of economic, biological, psychological and social theories. These have guided political, economic and social policies. And that is producing much social harm.

This phenomenon is rapidly spreading over the entire world through "globalization". Today the underpinnings of our social beliefs (our *zeitgeist*), is based on this seemingly "scientific" belief in materialism. This sets the tone for social interaction.

To materialist science, the properties of matter and its alternate form energy is all that need to be considered for any purpose. All benefit to society therefore is material. Social welfare depends on the ready availability of material goods. If this is true, then it should be proper that everyone should value material wealth above everything. Scientists have decided to believe that primordial life arose from matter by an accidental process when the chemical environment was right. It is also considered to be scientific belief that the evolution of man from primordial life occurred by different forms of life competing to acquire material advantages. Darwin's theory depends on that. The evolution of higher forms of life from the lower occurred by the survival of the fittest. In the materialist view the fit species is one which can acquire material advantages the best. Occasionally biologists have felt the need to explain such non-material things as love and compassion as leading to some form of fitness which makes a whole species rather than individuals more fit to acquire material advantage. Dr Dawkins[2] has described extensive game-theoretical calculations that he has made. This has led him to believe that society benefits most by the existence of a certain balance in the population between competitive and cooperative individuals. But even to him, such propensities to cooperation are mere instruments that lead to greater fitness to acquire material advantage for the specie.

But again, according to the materialistic view, such uneconomical behavior as compassion and cooperation in individuals leads to loss of wealth to the individual. The materialist sees no reason why exploitation of other humans and of nature should be discouraged in any way.

Moreover, this propensity towards competition is not something that can be controlled either. Each person in the materialist view is a machine driven by its own conditioned reflexes. There is no real existence in the individual's life of things like discipline, values and moral duty. One could thus describe the economic world as follows. It is an evolutionary process where these machines called humans compete for material wealth. This leads to evolution through "survival of the fittest" and "natural selection". With such a model, it is no surprise that society nurtures selfish people. Their headlong pursuit of profit would destroy one-another and destroy the natural world with all its riches. So "survival" leads ultimately to the destruction of the civilized world as we know it. This pursuit is based on the conditioned reflex of the Pavlovian dog. Long-term plans on the use of finite natural resources is allowed only if thoughts and feelings can be explained as high level conditioned reflex. And if as the leaders of society scientists see no way but to believe in the matter-centered, machine-driven world, that is the world we will get.

I am not dreaming up a caricature to make a point. The materialist view described here are actually espoused by influential people. Schumacher's "Small is Beautiful"[3] is one of the wisest books on economics I have ever read, but it is seldom quoted by mainstream economists, such is the wisdom of modern day economic theorists. The Quaker Economist Kenneth Boulding and his "grant theory" of economics[4] has also suffered similar fate. Schumacher has discussed in detail the way the distorted views of the materialist permeate the present economic system and the harm that has come from them. But nevertheless Daniel Dennett[5] argues with conviction, "Free will and moral responsibility are well worth wanting but the best defense of them must abandon the hopelessly contradiction-riddled myth of the distinct, separate soul". Another such purveyor of materialism is Ray Kurzweil, whose success in converting printed texts to sound has led to useful and profitable "reading machines". Kurzweil has extrapolated his success to expressing the faith that some day we will be able to design spiritual machines[6]. Marvin Minsky, author of "The society of the mind"[7] and one of the recognized "fathers of Artificial Intelligence" says he finds no problem with referring to us as, "Meat Machines". The recent publication of Christof Koch's, "The Quest for Consciousness"[8] has added grist to the same mill. Koch himself has not gone beyond claiming that he has found the Neural Correlate of Consciousness (NCC). This, of course, is different from the previous claim of people like Dennett, who think of consciousness as a mental construct or an epiphenomenon. But even the followers of NCC have not made any claims about anything beyond the neuronal correlate of what philosophers call "Qualia". These philosophers point out that the redness of an object is not encoded merely in the wave length of the light from it. It is our consciousness which gives it color. Koch has found that there are specific neuronal configurations that occur when a red object is seen. These are different from the configuration which sees a green thing. None of these findings, however, has anything to do with the later claims in this book. Indeed, Koch's findings are not qualitatively different from the findings by Warren McCulloch and his team in the early 70's[9] that the Frog's brain has neurons which fire when movement is seen, or when a curvature is perceived.

The brain certainly is the carrier of our thoughts – and Qualia can easily be the correlate of something in the brain. What we call, "Arithmetic done by a Computer" is the correlate of some mechanical interaction between electronic components. That has not led any psychologists to claim that a computer "knows" arithmetic. Correlates are just that – correlates. Correlation between Qualia and brain activities is in no way says that these activities "are" Qualia. Later on I shall indicate some other phenomena related to consciousness which have neuronal correlates also. Nevertheless, Koch's discovery has led his collaborator Dr. Francis Crick and some authors of popular reviews to claim that, "In the fullness of time educated people will believe that there is no soul independent of the body and hence no life after death". He was quoted in the New York Times[10]. And yet Dr. Oliver Sacks, himself a neuropsychologist of considerable fame, says, while discussing a patient[11], "Our cognitive sciences are themselves suffering from an agnosia essentially similar to Dr. P's. Dr. P. may therefore serve as a warning and a parable – of what happens to a science which eschews the judgmental, the particular, the personal and becomes entirely abstract and computational".

The author of Dr. Crick's quote also described Crick as having solved the mysteries of life. To use the accepted scientific criterion of repeatability, this should have enabled us to create life in a test tube. But we have only done it by placing a living cell into it – just placing a few molecules of DNA into it did not do the trick. And on the basis of this we can place life into the body? Maybe we can. But science certainly does not condone sweeping statements which transfer one area of inquiry into another. Such fairy tales make our later claims pale into insignificance in comparison.

Looking at Michael Lerner's claim[12] and the nature of materialism in science, I have come to a certain conclusion that I plan to share with the readers of this book. My thesis is that it is feasible and desirable for science to turn to a form of spirituality. However, such spirituality needs to be different from the every-day concept of God and religion, and should draw upon science itself as its source. And this spirituality in its turn needs to guide the future course of science, including the physical sciences.

To establish such a thesis I shall put forward an argument that it is possible to set up a belief system which does not contradict science but which accommodates the idea of extra-material entities and phenomena. I shall show that such a belief system actually removes some anomalies from science that exist to-day. Additionally, such a belief system opens Science to new avenues of development. I shall describe this form of spirituality in some detail. As I have said, this description will not be from the point of view of the normally accepted forms of religion. It will be much more from the point of view of science. This belief system removes materialism from a central position in science and frees society to pursue a spiritual path from which it becomes natural to argue for a society which encourages compassion and cooperation and which makes ecological balance an integral part of the social program.

CHAPTER 2.
Science and Spirituality

To many, including a large number of scientists, it seems ridiculous to juxtapose the terms Science and Spirituality. So to work up to what I want to say I will have to take very small steps. Each such step will involve a good amount of discussion. So let us get started.

(2a) The scientific method and the role of background beliefs.

Let us try to analyze what we mean when we say "the scientific method". I do not think any scientist will contradict me if I say that all scientific endeavors start with observing some phenomenon repeatedly under the same or different circumstances. The idea of observing it under the same circumstance is to find out whether the phenomenon changes. If it does, then of course, time itself is taken to be part of the circumstance. But let us say in the abstract that one finds that the phenomenon does not change when the circumstance does not change. Then one changes the circumstance and notes how the phenomenon changes. Then one tries to see if one can describe how the phenomenon depends on the circumstance.

Now, if one merely describes all the circumstances at which the phenomenon was observed and describes the phenomenon which occurred at that circumstance, one could make a rather large table of these "circumstance-phenomenon" pairs. This is actually done in the initial phase of a research. But then a more, somewhat less obvious step has to be taken. One constructs a rather small set of short statements about this relationship. These in themselves were not observed, but from these the phenomena at all the observed circumstances could be logically deduced. In fact, it can deduce the phenomena at circumstances which have not been observed yet – it can "predict" future occurrences of the relation. If these future occurrences are actually observed later, one says that these short statements are "verified". This set of sentences is called a "theory". People often call them "laws". Logicians call them "axioms".

How does one decide how to describe the circumstance and the phenomenon – what aspect of the phenomenon and the circumstance is worth paying attention to? This is a matter of judgment

– and judgment depends on "common sense", i.e. the prevalent beliefs of the times – scientific and social. Naturally, this common sense also influences the theories that are tried and developed. This fact will make a very useful starting point of my later arguments.

As time passes, the theories verified in the past gets incorporated into the common sense. But it also lends credence to the original common sense on which the theory was based. At that point any suggestion of changing the belief system may get wrongly interpreted as changing some existing theory.

I am saying all this to point out that people have started believing that materialism is a part of scientific theory. However, if one looks at all the basic laws of Science, one does not find any law which says that there can not exist any entity other than matter. Such a law is not necessary for predicting or exploiting any material phenomenon observed to this day. This reliance on matter is merely a reflection of the fact that most of successful science has dealt with phenomena exclusively dealing with matter. So there is a tendency in modern Biology, Psychology, and Sociology (of which Economics is a part) to emulate the very successful "hard sciences" (Physics, Chemistry). In these "soft" sciences also people try to explain all vital, mental and social phenomena in terms of properties of matter. As I just said, there is no theory in the hard sciences which justifies this. And this common sense of materialism gets reinforced when there is any evidence in these "soft" sciences that matter plays a significant role in the phenomena studied by them. This is because people consider materialism as the only basis on which things can be studied or even observed. We have already commented upon how Crick identifies Qualia with the Neuronal correlates of Qualia.

This may explain why theories in these soft sciences often are found to be wrong later. Just look at how many economic theories there are and how seldom their predictions come true. We have "Laissez faire" economics, Marxian economics, Keynsian Economics, Micro-Economics. All explain some physical aspect or other of the social phenomenon. That is what they were designed to explain. But none are patently successful in controlling human malaise. They are not even designed to do that. They just make the assumption that these physical phenomena are all that are needed to ease the malaise.

To illustrate this failing, let us realize that the recommendations of most economic theories are designed to optimize the total wealth of a nation. They completely neglect to analyze how their recommendations affect the distribution of that wealth. It looks like to them it is all right if all the wealth gets concentrated in a few hands, as long as the total wealth is great. The question of distribution becomes "someone else's responsibility". But these someone else must not upset the "economic" recommendations.

I must admit to having done some over-generalization here. In Keynsian economics, controlled capitalism with its progressive taxes have succeeded in distributing wealth more equitably. The United States benefited significantly with its experiments with this system till "supply-side" economics (basically Adam Smith's laissez-fare) took over. But even during the Keynsian era, social malaise could not be eliminated – merely covered over by an excessively zealous consumerism. The reason is not far to seek. Keynsian economics essentially nurtured the insecurity arising out of the "all for himself" philosophy he espoused. Schumacher quotes Lord Keynes as saying, "For another hundred years we must pretend to ourselves and to every one that fair is foul and foul is fair; for foul is useful and fair is not. Avarice and usury and precaution must be our gods for a little longer still".

I have already suggested that belief in materialism be removed from the belief system underlying science. But I need to point out that I am not suggesting that we eschew all future theory involving matter. The present axioms, laws and methods in the physical sciences have been quite successful in predicting the behavior of gross matter. This is true even if the grossness goes down to microscopic dimensions. Science is quite capable of handling most of the difficulties that arise in the way. My only warning here is that in handling future difficulties science should not continue to put itself into a materialistic strait jacket. Science may lead itself along very harmful paths if this is done. I shall presently indicate some difficulties that have not been handled yet. Also I have already said that applying materialistic biases to human affairs has already led to harm.

I agree that shedding materialism as a belief system will make a traumatic change in the approaches of science. However, there have been traumatic changes in the belief system in the past. These changes have actually advanced science into newer and more effective avenues. It may be a good idea at this moment to take two examples of the dependence of the scientific method on the prevailing belief system. What we are saying here is nothing new; Thomas Kuhn[13] has given a much more complete history of how these belief systems (he called them *paradigms*) form and change as science progresses.

In one case to be studied by us here the commonly accepted belief of the time seemed to work. In the other case it did not. The first, simpler case, where it worked, comes from a later period of time than the second, complicated case. And the study of the second case will also point out how spiritual matters got separated from science because of some historical reasons. And in the process the belief system at the basis of scientific thought changed.

(2b) Scientific investigations and change in mind set: early days.

The first example I am using is a prototype for the way work proceeds within an existing belief system. I am choosing this example because it is somewhat easy to understand and motivate.

Our story will start in the mid-1800s with a young Dane by the name of Hans Oersted, who conducted experiments linking electricity and magnetism. This work illuminated the path of later scientists like Michael Faraday of England. Faraday invented the electric motor and the dynamo. Let us see what kind of social atmosphere was prevailing to make Oersted's work possible.

By this time, both electricity and magnetism was known. Initially these were considered to be forces which were exerted by small electrified or magnetized regions of materials. Also, these were supposed to be essentially static phenomena. But later Galvani in Italy saw that this static charge can move from an electrified substance down a metal wire. In his case this electricity was used to activate the muscles in a frog's leg. So he called this phenomenon, "animal electricity" to differentiate it from static electricity. This nomenclature remained till another Italian, count Volta conducted experiments which produced electric currents without the use of animal tissues.

There was a bitter controversy between Galvani and Volta as to whether "animal electricity" is really related to the "life force". Volta's point of view prevailed and the idea of an electric current and means of producing it got understood and established.

Later on in our second story we shall see that such controversies between theories can lead to schisms and ultimately to a change of social belief systems. Compared to that the Galvani-Volta controversy was merely a scientific difference that could be resolved by experimental methods. No authority other than observation and experimentation was needed to be invoked to resolve the difference. No one seriously accused Volta of insulting the Creator of Life by contradicting Galvani. The present scientific method had already gained ascendancy. The Church did not put its oar in to make this into a theological controversy (our second story will shed some light on why this was).

Our story of Oersted had all this knowledge and understanding in the background.

Oersted was the follower of a philosophic school which held that all phenomena were descendants of one overall phenomenon. This, in a sense, was a belief system rather than a theory. It depended on opinions about what is "natural" rather than on observations. The University of Copenhagen had initially refused a chair to Oersted. They felt that Oersted was too much of a philosopher and not enough of a scientist. However, later Oersted did some impressive work on the relationship between electricity and chemistry. This won him a position and then a chair in Copenhagen University. Also this work indicated that his philosophic view was justified at least in the domain of chemistry and electricity. As we said earlier, his experiments on the relationship between electricity and magnetism was equally influential in setting the course of future research and their success. It might be worthwhile to describe these experiments. We shall do this in a formalized way to illustrate how the "scientific method" operates. This general approach to the scientific method has not changed to this day.

In his initial experiment Oersted connected the two ends of a battery with a piece of straight wire. Under the wire he placed a compass needle. When one battery end was disconnected, the compass pointed north as usual. But on making connection with the battery, the needle turned slightly and pointed away from the north. The effect was different than bringing the compass close to a piece of iron; the compass did not point towards the wire, but in a direction perpendicular to it. If the current was reversed by reversing the connection, the compass moved away from the north in the opposite direction. Bringing the wire below the compass instead of above, the direction of the compass changed again. It was not like something was attracting the pole of the compass. Rather it was like there was a force-field surrounding the wire to which the compass was responding. The force wrapped itself around the wire. Till then, electric and magnetic attraction was thought of as an attraction at a distance. Now people started thinking of electric and magnetic fields of force. In later times Clark Maxwell of England developed a set of exact equations connecting the two fields. His theory predicted the existence of electro-magnetic waves. The existence of such waves was experimentally verified by Heinrich Hertz in Germany and Jagadish Bose in India. Maxwell's theory was developed thus on the basis of the experiments of Oersted and Faraday.

Testing theories by observation and measurement had characterized science (then called, "natural philosophy") for a while before this. This way of doing things seems to make a lot of sense to us to-day. But in our next example we shall see how this point of view drew the wrath of the church in previous times. The resulting controversy led to a complete schism between science and religion. This schism influences peoples' thought even to-day. In many ways, this has been good. I have already commented on the pernicious things that have been and still are done in religion's name. This was true not just in the middle ages or in the middle east but is true even in modern "enlightened" America. That is why in my future discussion on the extension of science I shall not take a so-called "religious" point of view.

As I have said, our second example deals with the history of a schism between science and the church. This also was a controversy in science based on two kinds of "common sense" in Science. Galileo Galilei, born in Pisa in 1564 became the lightening rod in the schism.

People have had to observe the motions of the stars and the sun from the very early days of agriculture and ocean travel. A well accepted picture of the universe had emerged from these observations. People thought of two spheres. There was a very large one, containing the stars. There was also a spherical earth at the center of this celestial sphere. The starry sphere was in rotation around the pole star. Depending on where people were on earth, their horizon cut the north-south axis of this rotation at an angle. This gave the appearance of the stars rising in the east and setting in the west through the night.

However, this picture did not explain the way the sun rose and set at different times and at different places through the seasons. So the sun, as well as the planets were imagined to be situated somewhere between the two spheres and to have their own trajectories with respect to the stars.

In the West, this theorizing was initially the bailiwick of the Greeks. Ptolemy applied Euclid's geometrical methods to understand the motion of the sun and the planets in the sky. He used as common sense the obvious, observed fact that these bodies traveled around the earth just as the stars did. The sun seemed to move around among the stars once a year. Its axis of revolution was at a slight angle to the axis of the rotation of the stars. This gave rise to the variation of the length of the daylight hours and also to the seasons.

As can be seen, the Greeks did quite a good job of codifying the observations ("that star we call the pole star did not seem to move in the sky" "These other stars move, but the closer they are to the pole, the slower they seem to move -but they come back to the same place at about the same time every day" "the slight delay in their return to the same place depends on the season" and many, many others) into one overall, but rather simple theory.

However the motions of the Planets are sometimes slow, sometimes fast, sometimes forward, sometimes backwards. Some very complicated mathematical maneuverings were needed to explain them. We shall come back to these presently.

Ptolemy's geometry and his somewhat complicated models for the seemingly complicated motions of the planets went unchallenged for about two thousand years. Even the Church accepted him as the carrier of truth regarding astronomy. As so often happen, this accepted idea became in some ways the "word of God" (in those days, the Roman Church was the carrier of all western belief systems, including the scientific). Moreover, the idea that the skies revolved around the earth is reflected in many passages in the Bible – written with minds conditioned by what common sense called obvious in those days. In the 17th century a Pole by the name of Nicolaus Copernicus found that a much simpler theory of planetary motions could be developed. He assumed that the earth, as well as the planets actually traveled around the sun rather than everything traveling around the earth. The daily motion of the stars as well as these other bodies were due to the earth's spinning around its own axis. The apparent motion of the sun and the planets among the stars were due to the motion of the earth and the planets around the sun.

The calculations got much simpler. But how could one say that earth, the abode of man, God's beloved creation, was not the center of the Universe? This was almost like saying that God was not the center of the Universe. Copernicus himself was a canon of the church. So he needed to find support of his ideas among the ancient Greeks (including Pythagoras). He also had to make painstaking observations (instruments at the time were crude) and calculations so his idea would be taken seriously. He was a highly respected scholar and citizen and knew how much hostility his claim would generate. His book on the revolutions of heavenly bodies was not published till the year of his death. This was probably a fortunate accident for him. Moreover, the man who shepherded the book through the publication was careful to write a disclaimer in the preface. He said that what the author was suggesting was an easy method for calculation. It was not an actual claim about what moved where. So the church did not have to call him a heretic directly. They initially ignored his book. It was not till 20 years later that the book was placed on the list of proscribed books by the Roman Church.

But the mischief had been done. People who had been doing some of the calculations saw the simplicity of the calculations done by the Copernican model (they were still quite complicated for the layman, of course). The idea stayed even after the book was proscribed. Even some members of the Roman church felt that the difference between Copernicus and the Bible was more a matter of interpretation than anything else. At the time, Tycho Brahe was a young student in Denmark (and later, Germany). He started making detailed observations on the stars. He did not dare make the earth go around the sun, but still in his model, the planets did go around the sun while the sun went around the earth.

Around 1609, Galileo Galilei, a respected teacher and scientist in Italy, heard about a Dutch invention called a spyglass. He started calculations about the proper design of lenses to make the spyglass better and more powerful. Some spyglasses designed by him were put promptly into their spyglass business by Dutch businessmen. By this time the Copernican idea, if not totally accepted among scholars, had made quite an impact on their thoughts. Galileo, with his improved spyglasses started actually looking at the planets. And he saw the moons of Jupiter and how they actually went around Jupiter. He also found how the planet Venus, looked at closely, showed phases, just like the moon did in its rotation around the earth. This gave the Copernicans more evidence that the earth was not the center of the Universe. The Church, as the repository of all truths, could not ignore the controversy between the Ptolemeics and the Copernicans any more. To stay consistent with its previous Ptolemeic beliefs, the Church had to come down heavily on Galileo. Galileo was actually threatened with torture as a heretic. Under pain of these severe threats of punishment, and persuaded by his friends in the church, he had to agree not to make public statements about the matter. He even lied and said that he believed he was wrong in his previous writings. This started a major tension between what one would like to believe and what one actually saw.

At this point I would like to stop for a second and try to understand what I was saying when I said, "actually saw" in the last paragraph. The motion of the moons around Jupiter would look like a spiral motion if one added the motion of Jupiter with it. And if one believed in Ptolemy and thought of the moons as going around the earth then the moons of Jupiter also would be thought of as having a spiral motion around the earth. There was reason that Ptolemy could ignore the motions of the planets around the sun. The period of revolution of the planets was comparable to the period of the sun among the stars. Fortunately for Galileo, the motion of Jupiter was slower compared to the motions of its moons around it. So one could concentrate on the motions of the moons with respect to Jupiter. However, if one ignored looking at Jupiter and just looked at the moons one would "see" the moons as going around the earth in a complicated spiral motion. The difference of the points of view can not be resolved by mathematics, or even by observation. It depends on how one interpreted the mathematics and the observation. What the Copernicans were saying is that the mathematics would be much simpler to carry out if the motion of the planets were divided up into different motions. The motion of the sun "around the earth" (quoting Tych Brahe) was one. The motion of the planets (including Jupiter) around the sun was another. Then one considered the motions of the moons of Jupiter around Jupiter. From here it would not make much of a change if one explained the apparent motion of the sun as due to the motion of the earth around the sun. It is this latter picture which seemed the simplest, and hence the "true" picture to Galileo. The church, while investigating his heresy, had asked him to admit that while the earth was the center of the Universe, the sun, moons and planets revolved around it "as if" the earth and the planets revolved around the sun and the moons around the planets. And this he apparently agreed to do.

The Church's contention about Ptolemy's theory could have continued for some time, but for two things. Galileo himself, of course, kept saying to the board of Inquisition that he always thought of the Copernican scheme as a "Hypothesis" which he did not intend to hold or defend. But he had previously written so very strongly in favor of the Copernican hypothesis that there was little doubt that he believed in the correctness of Copernicus and the erroneousness of Ptolemy. Galileo told the Inquisition board that these were his human failings of arrogance which he abjured. But the rest of Europe was aware of his abilities as a scientist and mathematician and believed with him in the Copernican system. That belief led others to start asking detailed questions about the planetary orbits that would not even have been meaningful in the Ptolemaic system. Kepler, using Tycho Brahe's data, accurately calculated the elliptic shapes of the planetary orbits around the sun, as well as their speed along these orbits. Later, Newton's laws of motion and the law of gravity fitted exactly with these data – establishing Newton's theory as the basis of mechanics for the next two centuries (and, as a very close approximation, to this day). It is doubtful if these major progress would be possible if one followed the Church's contention that the Copernican model described the planetary motions around the earth "as if" they were around the sun. The Ptolemaic model could still be used to describe those spiral orbits. But by this time it became very difficult for the Church to ignore the progress in astronomical understanding. Eventually the Church had to cede the study of the world to science – that way it could continue its hegemony on matters spiritual.

I can not but iterate at this point the main point of what I want to say. Modern science can continue for quite a while acting "as if" matter is the only thing that exists. And that is the contention of most scientists to-day. However, I believe that the time is now ripe to change that belief system. We shall not discuss that in detail till the next Chapter, however. For the present let us continue with our stories.

I told the two stories (that of Galvani,Volta and Oersted and that of Ptolemy, Copernicus and Galileo) to establish two points. One point is that very often one can continue to do useful work on the basis of an established set of beliefs, as Galvani and Oersted did. The differences between Volta and Galvani, while contentious, was recognized as a difference between two theories, not as a difference in an underlying belief system. This kind of work increases one's confidence in the underlying beliefs. The other point is that it is possible to hold one set of beliefs as inviolate and continue to do believable work on these, as the Ptolemaic astronomers had done for centuries, without contributing to the progress of human understanding of the world. But it is also true that another set of beliefs could explain data equally well or better, more simply and leading to further useful work. The contending belief systems would give rise to different theories capable of describing existing data, however. What decides between the two belief systems is often people's mind sets. As we have said before, these mind sets were what Thomas Kuhn described in his book[14] as paradigms. And let me say once more that what I am arguing for is not a change in the theories but a change in the paradigm.

It is not clear that the Copernican system would have been accepted if the protestant revolution against the Roman Church was not in full swing during Galileo's time. The interest of the Dutch telescope makers in Galileo's continuing freedom may well have contributed to the Church's leniency towards Galileo. This leniency probably led to the great chagrin also of the protestants, who were equally vociferous in criticizing Copernicus.

Some may think that in modern times we have come past any possibility of any great change in sciences belief system. To counter that we shall move into the story of two such recent changes in the belief system of science in the next section.

These changes occurred with less social trauma than in the story of Galileo. But we still have some important questions to raise about the present state of science. Soon I shall suggest qualitative solutions to the unanswered questions of science and will have to face a trauma probably as great as that caused in Galileo's time. I shall discuss these. Then I shall suggest that we stop basing our theories on the centrality of matter but on the centrality of a much more abstract entity. My suggestion will have some relation to the mystic underpinnings of many religions. However, most so-called believers in "religion" generally ignore these mysticisms. So my suggestion may be as irksome to institutionalized religion as to conventional science.

(2c) Some recent changes in the mind set.

We have seen already that Maxwell's electromagnetic theory has been verified experimentally to everybody's satisfaction. It has led to the understanding that light is an electromagnetic wave, just like radio waves. The measured speed of light and that of radio waves have been found to be equal, adding to this conviction. This speed has turned out to be a constant in free space. In other media, it is modified according to the electrical and magnetic properties of the medium. This also is in accordance with previous theories regarding the bending of light beams by lenses. The science of light appears to be on a good footing.

But till about ninety years ago no one saw any need for asking questions like, "what is speed?" We all knew what that is: the space traversed in a given amount of time. But what is space and what is time? Again, we took for granted that we know what these are.

Perhaps people did realize that we have no real definition for time and space, but it did not seem to matter – our common sense worked pretty well. I remember I had a very wise teacher in college who started his course in dynamics by saying, "I will tell you everything about motions of bodies under all kinds of circumstances. But you must never ask me what is space and what is time. We will just assume that we all know what we mean by these words."

There was no problem with this attitude. Then two teachers in a technical college in Ohio, Professors Michelson and Morley, thought they had devised an experiment to measure the speed of the earth through space. We already knew with what speed the earth went around the sun. But we also realized that the sun was not stationary and had motion with the spinning Milky Way with respect to the stars. We had come a long distance from the days of Galileo. But the stars were moving too. All relative motions. So what was the *absolute* speed of the earth *through space* ? Of course, there was nothing known to be stationary in space. Thanks to Maxwell however, we knew that the speed of light through space was constant. Michelson and Morley decided to measure the earth's speed compared to the speed of light.

The idea was simple. To start the discussion, let us assume that we sent a beam of light towards a mirror in the same direction as the motion of the earth. As the light approached the mirror, the mirror would be moving away at the speed of the earth. So the light would reach the mirror a little bit later than it would if the earth was stationary. On its way back, this would be partially compensated by the fact that the receiving apparatus was moving towards the light. The total elapsed time between sending the light and receiving it back from the mirror could be calculated. We need of course to know the speed of the earth compared to the speed of light. A similar thing would happen if we sent the light perpendicular to the direction of motion of the earth: the light beam would go somewhat sideways to hit the mirror and to come back. The time taken could also be calculated.

Of course, neither of these times would be known in reality, since we did not know the direction the earth was moving through space. Nor could we know what the difference would be between the two times of arrival of the two perpendicular beams. But we do know that as we turned this whole measuring system (the sender, receiver and mirrors) around, the difference would have different values in different directions. If the earth were stationary, this value would be the same, no matter in what direction the system was placed. But if the earth was moving and we turned the system around, this difference would wax and wane with the angle. From the amount of this variation one could calculate the speed of the earth through space.

What they found to their surprise was that there was no difference in the speed in the two different directions. They thought that perhaps the speed of the earth around the sun , the speed of the sun with respect to the galaxy and the motion of the galaxy in space were canceling each other out. So they repeated the experiment six months later, when the earth would be moving in the opposite direction with respect to the sun. They still did not see any speed. Einstein's special theory of relativity arose to explain this failure of the experiments of Michelson and Morley to measure the speed of the earth through space. Instead of trying to "explain" this failure, Einstein decided to investigate logically what our concepts of distance, time, speed and other physical quantities would be like if the speed of light relative to any platform of observation was indeed a constant. With such modified concepts anybody who measured the speed of light standing on any platform would find the same speed whether the platform itself was moving or not. Any speed we wanted to measure could only be speed relative to another platform of observation. Once Michelson and Morley's result was accepted as correct, the concepts needed to be recast in a rather drastic way. It took science some time to wean itself from the belief that space and time were separate and absolute. This belief about the distinction between space and time was not based on any scientific construct but merely on prevalent "common sense". To this day that common sense distinction between space and time forms the common sense of everybody.

Science did not have too much difficulty in accepting the new view of space and time. Scientific "common sense" incorporated the view that space and time were merely different "directions" in a four-dimensional space (This is often called the Minkowski space-time). Each observer saw time to be flowing along a specific direction. But another observer, moving with a certain speed with respect to the first observer saw time as moving along a different direction. The first observer was seen as merely moving through space along a direction which is not quite square with the second observers time. The time that the first observer saw looks to the second observer as perpendicular to the direction of motion of the first observer through space.

This certainly is not the common sense entertained by the man in the street. But the scientist understands the common "wrong" view as merely the result of the fact that most of us move relative to each other at a very small speed compared to the speed of light so the very small difference in the directions of our times are too small to be measured by any but the most sensitive measuring instruments. The Physicist George Gamow[15] once wrote a very interesting story book describing what happens in a world where the speed of light is ten miles an hour. Things indeed turn bizarre in such a world.

There has also been another rather jarring change in "common sense" that has been forced on scientists – one that has left its reverberation to this day. Scientists have gotten used to doing their calculations according to a new theory of matter and light promulgated about 70 years ago. But they still feel uncomfortable about the world view (Common sense) on which this new theory of matter and light is based. Let us look at this new theory and the kind of common sense indicated by it.

This new theory became necessary when a number of different experimental results about the building blocks of matter raised questions about the correctness of the "classical" views of physics – the physics of Newton and Maxwell. At the same time, other experiments on the behavior of light also were leading to very similar puzzlements. We shall say a few words about both of them. It will be noted that in this case also as in the case of the Michaelson-Morley experiments, Albert Einstein, like Galileo of old, was among the precursors of our new view of matter. Fortunately with the church out of the picture at this point, he received accolades rather than threats.

By the mid 1800s , it was agreed that all substances were built of small particles (the "molecules") which in their turn were built of smaller particles, the "atoms". While there are millions of substances, there are only ninety-odd kinds of atoms from which the molecules of all substances are built. In those days, the building blocks of atoms were thought to be three kinds of particles. There were the two heavier particles, protons and neutrons and the much, much lighter particles, the electrons. The protons and neutrons were tightly clustered together in the "nucleus" of the atom and the electrons went round the nucleus like the planets going around the sun. The different elements were different in the charges carried by the nucleus, i.e. the number of protons there were in them. The number of electrons going around in the atoms were equal to the number of protons in the neucleus so the atom was electrically neutral.

We shall not go into the details of the experiments that established this picture firmly as correct. Let us just say they were. But it is also beyond doubt that this picture flies straight into the face of Maxwell's theory of electro-magnetism. The problem lay in the fact that the curved paths that the electrons followed around the nucleus would force them to emit electro-magnetic waves. Some of these would be light. There would also be some other kinds like radiant heat, ultraviolet, etc. The kind of waves emitted would depend on the distance of the electron's orbit from the nucleus. Also, the loss of energy caused by this radiation would force the electrons to spiral closer to the nucleus. The new orbit would radiate lights of different colors. Thus atoms would spontaneously radiate a whole spectrum of colors (like sunlight as seen though a prism). Ultimately the electrons would collapse into the nucleus, ending the life of the atom. All elements would be short-lived. But this certainly is contrary to what happens. Most elements are stable substances. Moreover, they do not emit any radiation unless they are disturbed in some way, like heating, or being hit by external electron beams (like in a neon-tube). And when they are disturbed, they do not emit light in a rainbow pattern. They emit distinct colors, well-separated from each other. There was a theory of sorts that explained all this, but that theory was on very shaky grounds, and entirely at odds with all of classical physics.

To resolve these difficulties scientists had to develop an entirely different theory of matter and energy, the new Quantum theory. To get an idea of this new theory we need to study in some detail the nature of light waves (or any other wave, including waves in water). We will also have to consider some experiments on the production of electricity by shining light on certain materials (the basis of the construction of solar panels and digital cameras). Let us look at the first and more complicated issue, the nature of waves.

First thing about waves on water – in a wave, some part of the water is high, some part is low. These high and low parts (called "crests" and "troughs") follow each other as the wave proceeds through the water. The water does not move as much as the wave moves – water just moves up and down as the crests and troughs go through. Actually, if the distance between two crests (the "wave length") is m feet and the speed of the wave (not the water!) is s feet per second, then the water moves up and down s/m times every second. This number of up and down motions per second is called the "frequency". So the speed of the wave is equal to the product of the wave length and the frequency. A very important formula in Physics – but the idea is really simple.

If the wave is not in water but in air (like in sound waves) the motion of the medium (water in the last paragraph, air here) is forward-and-back instead of up and down – giving rise to a wave of compressed and rarified air. In an electro-magnetic wave it is the direction of the electric and magnetic fields which changes instead of the up-and-down motion. But the basic idea is the same.

Let us now imagine a piano tuner at work. He has a source of sound called a tuning fork which hums with a fixed frequency (here we call it the pitch). He uses it to make sure that the piano wires are in tune. For our purpose, let us say that he is trying to tune a specific wire (generally the middle C) to have the same pitch as the tuning fork. When his wire is very close to "in tune" he can tell the exact difference between the pitch of the wire and that of the tuning fork by listening for a slow waxing and waning of the sound when the two notes are sounded together. These waxings and wanings are called "beats". They happen because the sound waves from the wire and the fork "interfere" with each other. The phenomenon is very similar (and somewhat easier to understand) if instead of two close notes, we think of two water waves coming from two sources close to each other (one can produce this effect by throwing two stones in the water very close to each other). We find that the water shows two waves spreading from the two points; but in the region where the two waves overlap, some "dead zones" develop where there is no motion of the water. The reason for this is as follows.

First let us consider a point at equal distance from the sources. When the crest of the wave from one source reaches this point, the crest from the other wave also arrives. The heights of the water add and we get a crest twice as high as the crests of the two separate waves. Now let us move over to a point whose distance from the two sources are such that when the crest from one source reaches it, the other wave has had time to bring a trough to the same point. The two "add" – the rise of the water due to one wave cancels the fall of the water from the other and we have no motion of the water at all.

The same thing happens in sound waves, as we have hinted above. It also happens in electro-magnetic waves like light.

We went through this song and dance because the phenomenon of wave interference has played a historical role in our understanding of nature at several points of history. The first time was when people were wondering about the nature of light. It was known that light travels in a straight line (think of a ray of sunbeam entering a dark room through a crack in the shutters). But Newton had already postulated that particles travel in straight lines also (his famous "first law of motion" – amply verified by then). So it was natural for Newton to suggest that light consists of stream of tiny particles. But others pointed out that waves travel in straight lines too (let water waves pass through a slit in a barrier and this will become visually obvious). Moreover, people did find some evidence that just like waves, light does go around corners (place a stick in water and see the wave go around it). So experiments were conducted to see if light interferes just like waves do. A definitive experiment was somewhat hard to perform since the wave length of light is much smaller than that of water and sound waves that we have been thinking of. So the sources would have to be quite close, and this was hard to achieve.

An Englishman by the name of Thomas Young succeeded in designing experiments to detect interference of light (the famous "Young's double-slit") in the early 1800's. Light was found to interfere like waves. The wave nature of light was well accepted by the mid-1800's. The exact theory of wave interference was developed by the Dutch mathematician Huygens and French Mathematician Fresnel. The wave theory of light remained unchallenged from then till this century.

It is this "common sense" about light that led Maxwell to postulate that light also was an electromagnetic wave. But after a while after this the phenomenon of photo-electricity was discovered.

The phenomenon called photo-electricity is what is responsible for the workings of TV cameras, digital cameras and solar cells. What happens is that certain materials emit electricity (i.e streams of electrons) when illuminated with light. The energy of the light knocks electrons out of the atoms of the material involved. However, the electrons do not get knocked out by just the light of any color whatever. Colors closer to red (i.e. colors of longer wave length or lower frequency) do not knock out electrons since they do not have enough energy or "kick". This is true no matter how strong or bright the light is – just a lot of energy does not work. Even faint light of sufficiently high frequency will produce an electric current, albeit feeble. Given this color, the strength of the electric current would be higher the brighter the light.

This puzzling behavior can be explained if we assume that light consists of particles ("photons") whose energy depends on the frequency of the light – the more the frequency the higher the energy. The energy has to be high enough to knock the electrons out of the atoms. If the beam is strong, then of course more electrons will be knocked out – but to kick even one electron out of the atom needs a minimum energy in each individual photon.

Looks like that while light travels as a wave, it is absorbed as particles. The particle nature of light had already been postulated a few years earlier to explain certain anomalies of the color of light emitted by black bodies. Photo-electricity corroborated that supposition. But so far it had always been thought that particles, in their motion, obey Newton's laws of motion. Light particles obviously did not. Light particles travel as waves. But how can they? Do the particles break up and become waves and then congeal together when they hit the photo-electric material? That would be absurd – how would the particles "know" when it is time to congeal? Do they remain waves if the material does not respond to its frequency?

This difficulty can be resolved (at least partially) and we soon will resolve it. But before that let us go back to electrons and look at their behavior. It had already been observed that electrons behave like particles. There are ways to make paths of electrons visible (in "cathode ray tubes" and in the TV tubes). And it had already been seen that these rays move in straight lines. Moreover, if an electric field is placed perpendicular to the path of electrons, the path bends under the electric force just as Newton's laws predict. However, when the peculiar nature of light particles were discovered, people thought of finding out how electron beams behave when they pass through Young's double slit (see above). And behold, electron beams show interference just like light beams. Here are another bunch of particles which move under Newton's laws when subjected to large scale experiments like passing them through electric or magnetic fields, and act like waves when sufficiently fine experiments like the double slit experiment is performed on them. Why are these particles trying to confuse our understanding?

In the next part of our discussion we shall attempt a resolution of the problem. To some the resolution will seem "perfectly satisfactory". Our view, however, is that the resolution leaves a little bit to be desired – and this will lead us to suggest a new belief set. To some it will be "unscientific", but our belief is that this is only because Science is poised at the threshold of a new kind of "common sense" which will not only allow science to move into new uncharted directions, but will lead to a much superior basis for a just, compassionate and healthier society.

CHAPTER 3.

The Quantum Physicist and the Nature of the World - the Mystic's approach to the nature of existence.

We came to a dilemma at the end of the last Chapter. Our experience about very small particles – especially electrons and photons – has led us to believe that these particles show a dual behavior: sometime they behave like particles and sometimes they behave as waves. Even some textbooks of Physics, especially those written for secondary schools (where there is a need to oversimplify the mathematics) have tried to wrap this matter in somewhat confusing language like, "they are particles if you look at them as particles and they are waves if you look at them as waves". Hardly a scientific statement by modern standards.

Physicists do not need to use this kind of language, and in reality they do not. To resolve the dilemma, they need merely to point out that just because something is a particle, it does not mean that its motion needs to obey the laws of motion established by Newton. Actually, just as Einstein's laws of motion can be quite nicely approximated by Newton's laws when the particles move slowly enough, so can the laws of motion deduced from the new Quantum Mechanics be approximated by Newton's laws, when the particles involved are heavy enough. Also, the Quantum laws of electromagnetic waves approximate to Maxwell's laws when the wave lengths are much larger than that of light – say as in the case of radio and television waves. Let us discuss these laws now.

We have been constantly using the analogy of water and sound waves in our discussions in the previous sections. However, we shall now point out that the analogy becomes too crude when it comes to the motion of photons and electrons. The nature of Quantum theory is such that although for large particles and long waves they approximate the laws of classical (i.e. Newtonian and Maxwellian) Physics, they actually use an entirely different "common sense". Small particles which move fast enough have their position predicted by laws different from Newton's laws. Instead these laws, instead of predicting the exact position of the particles, merely predict the chance (the "probability") that the particle be at specific positions. The stronger the wave is at a point, the higher the chance that the particle would be there. Instead of saying that at a certain time the particle will be at position x (as Newton's laws would say), the law says that the chance of the particle being very far from x is very small and the chance of its being very close to x is very high. Where it will actually be depends on the specific instance – if one performs the experiment many times, in a very few cases it will be far from x; in most cases it will be very close to x, even exactly at x.

The situation is very similar to that faced by insurance companies when they determine the premium for a person's life insurance. On the basis of long experience, they know the chance of a person living to different ages. So they can predict the chance of their losing money when paying the person's dependants on the person's death. The longer he lives, the more the money the company makes from his premiums. If he dies earlier than expected, the company loses money paying the benefits.

Insurance companies, who have a large number of clients, have no problem with this kind of uncertainty. What they lose on one client who dies early, they more than make up on another who lives long. They fix the premiums based on their average gain over many clients and they come out fine. Similarly, electronic engineers can predict what thickness of semi-conductors will make the most useful electronic components. This is because they know the quantum mechanical probability of electrons moving against voltage fields. They are dealing with enough electrons in a computer or a radio so the uncertainty does not bother them.

So electronic engineers and applied Physicists are quite happy with Quantum Mechanics as it stands today. In what follows we shall deal with the problem as it appears to a pure Physicist. His job is not to make devices to sell at a profit. His job is to understand the nature of the real world.

Newton believed that he knew how particles move. Within the experience of the scientists and engineers of the day, there was no reason to question his belief. But does the Quantum Physicist know how particles move?

To a certain approximation they do, as we have already seen above. When it comes to large streams of particles, they can feel confident about themselves. But if one points to a particle and ask, "Where will this particle be a microsecond from now?" they need to hedge.

We have already seen a comfort among engineers analogous to the comfort in the insurance business. Let us now think of the doctor talking to his patient in his office. He can not say, "the chances are more than 80 percent that you will be alive 5 years from now, so don't worry. That will be $125, please". He will not be considered a very desirable doctor. So he has to look for the factors that affect an individual. He may take blood tests, he might ask him about his state of health and his family history, he might prescribe medicines and worry about its side-effects. But what does the physicist look at in a particle? On what basis can he answer questions about it except for predicting probabilities? Unlike the doctor, he does not have a clue.

There are various conundrums known to the physicists about this lack of knowledge. A rather poignant one is the following[16]. Let a small amount of radioactive material be placed in a container in a device. In the device any radioactive emission starts a current through a circuit. The current activates a motor which drops a pellet of cyanide into a trough of acid. This would emit a very poisonous gas that would kill a cat tethered next to the trough. The amount of radioactive material is small enough so the probability of an emission during an hour is about half and half. We enclose the whole system into a closed opaque box. If we open the box in an hour, will the cat be alive or dead? Of course, we shall know if it is dead when we open the box. But what can we say just before we do that? We can not know, for sure – but it will be one of the two, alive or dead. Does its being alive or dead depend on our knowing? And even if we say that the cat gets killed by our act of observation, could it also happen that a dead cat is brought alive by our act of observation?

There are Physicists who feel that the question is irrelevant. Quantum Mechanics tells us the way our knowledge is reflected in our observation. If there is no previous knowledge then it is truly unknown what the observation will reveal till the observation is made. As long as the observation is not made, its existence is not relevant.

In any case, it looks like the crux of the matter lies in a conscious observation. But what IS the phenomenon of observation? Certain excitement in some brain, right? But that in itself is an uncertain statement – a brain cell is a material substance subject to the laws of Quantum theory. So its behavior itself is uncertain. How does the act of observation bring a possibility into a reality?

Materialists have so far refused to answer this question, resorting instead to silence. They believe that someday we will get an answer to this question. And any answer not based on something material will not be accepted. So let us wait – and perhaps wait some more – and then some more. Just as the statistics of a patient's mortality becomes a reality when the Physician knows more about what is going on in the patient's body, so some "hidden variable" will someday be found which determines the reality.

And this "hidden variable" must not only explain how the radioactivity occurs at the moment of observation so the cat dies. It must also explain why the dead cat is observed by the simultaneous excitation of a certain brain state in the observer.

One hidden variable seems to be this thing in the observer called "consciousness". Some very eminent scientists have been trying to unravel the source of this consciousness in the brain. The consensus seems more and more to be that there is really nothing called consciousness. There is only mechanical response to stimulus. The stimulus and response may be of more and more complex kind. At a certain (so far un-understood) level of complexity these responses appear in the subject's mind as self-consciousness. And this apparent thing is what changes the probability of the cat's death to actuality? The neuroscientists who have called consciousness a hallucination have not explained the cat's life or death question. Nor have the adherents of Neural correlates of consciousness that we talked about in Chapter 1.

We shall leave the materialist with their waiting game and with the inhuman kind of society they seem to predict, as we have seen earlier. Let us see if we can make some progress towards this problem of existence (as opposed to the probability of existence) by invoking something nonmaterial. Our understanding in this matter is bound to be rudimentary. Very few serious scientists have taken this point of view seriously enough to further this understanding. I first found a scientific discussion of the resolution of this problem in a book[17] by Amit Goswami, a professor of Physics at the University of Oregon.

Goswami has so far been treated with either derision or almost complete neglect by the scientific community. The reason for this is that Scientists have this "common sense" which says that believing in anything other than matter is some kind of a stupid "sin". Meanwhile, the basis of Goswami's understanding has been a basic tenet of some Eastern Philosophies for about four thousand years.

At this point of our discussion we shall not go into how these old philosophers came to their conclusion. Instead we shall start with just one basic axiom on which they started their discussion. Whether their discussions will be ratified by modern scientific methods is once more a thing for the future. It is possible that the methods used for this ratification will not be confined to the materialistic methods we know at present. We will only claim initially that the conundrum we have been given by Quantum Mechanics can be resolved by adding just one axiom to those of present day science. Then we shall attempt further developments of that point of view.

This new axiom ("theory" if you will) is that there is a thing, which I shall call "consciousness", which can act on the potential existence of particles (as described by Quantum Mechanics) and bring it to a reality. At this stage we shall not try to unravel how among the many possible positions of a particle just one will be chosen.

We do not know enough about the properties of this consciousness yet. But just this one axiom at least explains the existence of real (as opposed to probable) particles.

Is this consciousness in any way related to what we call consciousness in living beings? Is it the same consciousness as that of the observer which is required to observe a quantum phenomenon as a real phenomenon? This question we shall answer with a "yes" without having to invoke any property of consciousness other than what we have already invoked, i.e that consciousness exists and that it can bring potential existences to real existence. What we will invoke is a certain philosophical insight into the nature of observations or perceptions. Also we shall invoke certain quantum mechanical properties of brain cells that scientists have discovered. Let us do all this in a separate Chapter.

CHAPTER 4.

"Universal Consciousness" and "individual consciousness" in the phenomenon of observation.

Let us go back to one of the points we discussed in the last chapter: that material objects can be said to exist only when they are consciously observed. So any time anything is known to exist, two separate things are needed. The observed object which has come into existence is needed. The observation mechanism used by the conscious observer is also needed. The observation mechanism may involve various material objects, including measuring devices like scales, voltmeters and optical devices like microscopes, telescopes or cameras. Eventually however, it all ends up with the human eye, ear, skin, nose or taste. These are invariably backed up by the brain of course. The entire chain of materials involved in an observation, including the observed object or event and the brain has to have their quantum potential collapsed to reality at the same time. But none of these things give rise to the observation. There has to be this consciousness somewhere that separates the observer from the observed. It is not an impersonal, "This is seen". It has to be "I see this". Now the consciousness that brings about this separation between "I" and "this" can not be the universal consciousness which collapsed all the matter involved in the observation. The "I" is attached to the observer, as opposed to the observed. The universal consciousness that collapsed all the material involved in the observation is separate from both the observer and the observed. So where is the consciousness coming from that makes the "I"? As we have said above, the materialist[18] says, "There is no I". And this non-entity makes the difference between the live and the dead cat of the last chapter?

We have already have had occasion to discuss the work of Koch and Crick who have discovered neural correlates of consciousness. But this throws us back to the same old quantum mechanical question that Koch and Crick has not discussed: how does the material brain come into existence when all science can predict about it is the probability of its existence? We are still left with the question of the nature of the relationship between Universal and Individual consciousness.

Let us for a moment give credence to our own subjective, private belief that each one of us know that he or she is conscious. Clearly, the discussion above indicates that we do not get an acceptable explanation for that phenomenon from materialistic science. It may not be unreasonable then to see if the Eastern Philosophies can bail us out of this, as it did by supplying the hypothesis of the universal consciousness. Unfortunately, we do not get a clear answer there either. Some schools of philosophy hold that only the universal consciousness is real and that individual consciousness is an illusion (i.e. a epiphenomenal construct of the neural system, as Dennett suggests). But there are also others who hold that individual consciousness is an entity distinct from the universal consciousness. Instead of looking at a possible rapprochement between these two views, we shall follow Goswami's lead from science and look for a mechanism by which the neural system can bring about a seeming separation between universal and individual consciousness. Let us delve back into a little bit of Quantum Mechanics again.

As we have seen before, when a body is massive enough, the quantum mechanical probability of its existence at any instant is heavily concentrated at some specific point of space. As a result it always appears to be moving according to Newtonian laws any time it is observed. This becomes apparent when one uses a large number for the mass in the quantum equation of a moving body. But that is not the entire story, is it? After all, every massive object is made up of tiny particles which in themselves move probabilistically according to quantum laws. However, when they are closely knit, acting upon each other with their inter-particle forces, the totality of them acts like a massive particle. At least, that is how it appears from their behavior and from the quantum mechanics of massive particles. But the actual mathematics of the quantum mechanics which makes an assemblage of small particles act like a big one is exceedingly complex. People have started to make inroads into this only recently. Here we shall only talk about one such effort – applied to brain cells – which sheds some light into the question of individual consciousness.

A brain cell is much larger than a fundamental particle like an electron or a photon. So it is not entirely governed by quantum laws of motion. But then, a brain cell is not so large that one can ascribe Newtonian properties to its motion either. So how does one deal with such an intermediate phenomenon? One can simplify the mathematics we referred to above by making an approximation. One can modify the usual quantum equations by adding an extra term (mathematicians would say, "a non-linear term") to the quantum equation. Even the somewhat simple resulting equation is hard to solve in exact form. Goswami and his student Mitchell[19] solved the equation by approximate, numerical methods and found that a particle governed by such an approximate equation shows a form of memory. Any time the particle governed by such an equation collapses to a reality at a certain instant, its subsequent quantum motion has a higher probability at the point of previous collapse. Thus such particles, instead of collapsing at the points according to the quantum randomness, has a tendency to follow its previous paths. Its behavior pattern becomes more habitual the more often it is collapsed. Any time consciousness collapses it, it has a greater tendency to collapse in ways to which it is habituated. It modifies consciousness according to its own "nature" so to speak. Thus the consciousness associated with a brain is a modified form of universal consciousness. That is where it becomes conscious of a separation from the rest of the world phenomenon. It is this idea which is often described to be the "soul" of the individual. It is not a material object, it is a tendency of matter to act in specific ways. The phenomenon can also be referred to as the tendency of an individual entity to react to events according to its predisposition.

This theory seems to indicate that if someone can recognize ones predispositions as arising from a purely mechanical process and can disassociate oneself from one's desires and predilections, one can identify ones consciousness with the universal consciousness.

This identity of the individual consciousness and the universal consciousness may seem a little illogical. The individual consciousness is less free to act in random ways than the universal consciousness. Is it then logical to call them the same? It is this argument, in some form or other, which motivates some people into thinking that these two are distinct. On the other hand, it is not clear that all things that exist have to be subject to air-tight logic.

This last sentence may raise some eyebrows. Is it not logic which has guided all human endeavors? Scientists seem to believe so. But we have already seen that their logic based on materialism does not take into account the existence of sociological and ecological ethics in any satisfactory way. That is what motivated me in the first place to look for a non-materialistic theory of the world. So the question that looms here is, do we have to abandon logic the same time we abandon materialism? I am not entirely convinced of this: the exact logical form of the arguments about consciousness has never been studied precisely. This is certainly an area where precise logical calculations are needed.

But as an aside I personally would not be entirely upset if logic had to be abandoned at some future date. Because it is the logicians themselves who have discovered that no finite logical system can explain all properties of all phenomena. They have proved that any time one proposes a logical system of belief, one can raise a question which can not be answered with either a "yes" or with a "no" with that system.

It is not clear to me whether this is a matter which I need to enlarge on at this point with more explanation. So let me continue with another part of the discussion, leaving the question of logicality for an appendix. However, all this discussion has not refuted the claim that the axiom of Universal Consciousness is needed for the Ontology of Quantum Mechanics. All our argument about logicality of the identity of the Individual and Universal Consciousness was merely a question for future research – perhaps even logical research.

At this point I would like to claim that I have established the first point that I wanted to establish in this book. I have pointed out how one can add one extra axiom into science which will enrich science without changing anything in science that we have built so far. In addition, it does have something to say about one central ontological problem which Schroedinger (see endnote 16) so ably illustrated by his story of the cat.

But I have not even have begun a discussion of the second point I raised at the beginning. Our discussion has indicated that if we remove materialism from the belief system of science, then we need not build the kind of harmful social theories that we have built. The fulfillment of individual desires does not remain central in the idealist system, i.e. where universal consciousness is known to be the only reality. But can we develop an ethical social theory just by positing the existence of consciousness as basic to the world? Actually, our extra axiom does not force one to incorporate ethics into our new belief system. There are plenty of people - in India as elsewhere - who believe in the idealist approach, but find it satisfactory just to withdraw from the world of desires into a life of ascetism and isolation from the world. But suppose one does not find it possible in one's predisposition to isolate oneself from the world. In what way would our theory be of benefit to him? For him we need an argument to include ethics into our theory.

To do that we need to extend our theory considerably. We shall have to add at least one more axiom into the theory. We shall have to bring in certain ideas from biology and chaos theory. To introduce and motivate such an exercise, I have decided to start our discussion by referring to an old experimental observation, which leads to an ethical view of life. This experiment has been carried out by people who believe in the correctness of our theory of consciousness. We shall describe that experimental observation first, and then try to explain that observation. This will lead to some required changes both in our social theories and in the theory of evolution. On the way we will have to introduce a concept which may be called God. That concept will probably ring a bell with mystics of every religion. It will probably also incur the wrath of many established institutions which call themselves religious. To me, that is one reason I like the concept.

Let us go on with this, again in small steps.

CHAPTER 5.

Experiments on the Universal Consciousness: the Budddhist concept of "Karuna".

The idea of the universal consciousness as the basic source of the world was developed very early in history in the East. It forms the basic underpinning of both Hinduism and Buddhism. The Hindus later on embellished that idea, and finally attracted into its body various different lines of religious thought, becoming what it is to-day. The Teravada or Hinayani Buddhists have carried on their experiments on the basic philosophy in its pure form. The Mahayani Buddhists, like the Sankhya school of Hindus accepted individual consciousness as distinct from the universal consciousness. Their thoughts went from there to Gods and Goddesses, just as did many sects of Hindus. We shall try to stick with our single hypothesis and follow the Hinayani Buddhists with their experiments.

Now at a first glance it seems that it should be easy to carry out experiments on consciousness according to our theory. After all, it is our own consciousness that we are talking about. But the difficulty is that our brain constrains consciousness to move along paths determined by our past experience. It is not the unfettered consciousness that creates matter. The only way to cut through our limited, conditioned consciousness is to recognize the preconditioning for what it is. We are sufficiently complex organisms to be capable of introspection and to be able to control our thoughts. The Buddhists specify meditational practices to enhance our abilities in this direction. At least for a limited amount of time and to a certain extent, these practices lead us to the universal consciousness in us. The underpinning of the social structure we have been hinting at is based on the experience of people who can achieve this, to the extent that they can describe them. It will take us a while to get to the theoretical basis for that. For the present we shall merely repeat their description of the experience.

A major component of the experience of accomplished Buddhist practitioners is "Karuna". The word translates roughly to "compassion", the ability to feel other people's joys and sorrows as ones own. But here the word may also include the idea of understanding. By understanding we mean the understanding of the fact that the difference between people - and between people and animals and things – is merely the difference in the way our consciousness is constrained. Fundamentally, all of us are the manifestation of the same consciousness.

This result of the Buddhist experience does not quite follow the methods of observation dictated by science. The experience is personal and individual. But the experience is shared by at least a limited number of people. Later on we shall have occasion to discuss this matter in detail as we discuss our extended science. For the present, we shall just posit that this result obtained by the Buddhist meditators is valid.

Now it is our common experience that we all want to continue our existence and to flourish in whatever way we desire. To the extent that such desires can be satisfied they can be a source of pleasure. But the desires may be in contradiction of the laws of nature. Some of these laws are known to science, but there may be more to the laws of nature. A person with Karuna understands these other laws better than most of us. But the person with Karuna can also sympathize with the pain that may accrue to people if their desires are not fulfilled. The person with Karuna would also want to help such people. This is done either by supporting them in their efforts to fulfill their desires or explaining to them in what way the desires and the efforts should be modified to fit reality. In his or her Karuna he or she can also realize the best way that the people can be taught to shun or achieve their desired state. Stories about the Buddha abound with accounts of the ways the Buddha used to accomplish such helps.

An accomplished Buddhist practitioner also understands the place of every living and non-living object in the total scheme of creation. These outcomes of Karuna formed the basis of the social teachings of Buddhist and Taoist teachers.

If we accept the above statements to be true then the resulting social and ecological basis of society is entirely different from the materialist picture we have looked at. The root of all existence is not matter but consciousness. This consciousness is accessible to all but the access path is difficult. Those who can access it understand that our physical existence is a secondary phenomenon. No person is more important than another person or another thing. One's own existence is ephemeral and unimportant. However, as long as one exists one has pleasure and pain. The wise know that everybody's pleasure and pain has equal importance. So one should try to believe and feel this also. Such wisdom brings freedom from the pain that comes from attaching importance to one's desires. Thus one's greatest pleasure should come from allaying the pain and enhancing the pleasure of everyone, including oneself. This takes compromises and balances, but that is the balance that leads us towards freedom.

Let me leave the reader to imagine what kind of a social structure arises naturally from such a world view. The entire picture is filled with difficult balancing acts – everyone does not have the same definition of pleasure. One needs to look at the future as well as the present. It takes long and arduous discussion in society as one proceeds to an ideal acceptable to all. The need for acceptability is a part of the compassion that the wise tell us to have.

This approach to the world certainly is not to the liking of those who believe that making money or buying cars or becoming famous or seducing sex-objects is the goal of life. Nor will it sit well with people who think that they know the truth and take it upon themselves to force people to accept that truth. So one needs to change the social belief system. Once people believed that the religious leaders are the only claimants to wisdom and knowledge. They set the tone for social and economic interaction. When these leaders had wisdom of sorts, things went well. If the leaders were corrupted, then their influence was the source of great social harm and injustice.

My belief is that scientists have that position of leadership to-day. And that is why I believe that scientists should change their belief system to be consciousness-centered rather than matter centered. That may lead society towards more humane practices without distorting existing science. It may even enrich science into pursuing new directions of investigation.

There would be aberrations, of course. Even to-day there are scientists who tilt their research results in favor of their bosses. The Pentagon has encouraged many scientists to investigate the possibility of mind control. But the culture would have a different base then and such aberrations would be much less attractive.

I hope at this point I shall not be accused of teaching Buddhism, because I am not. But in the past I have claimed that there is an extension of science that can not only remove the harm brought about by materialism but can actually lead to a social theory based on compassion and ecological wisdom. The only way I could justify the latter claim without going into another long theoretical discussion on the manifestations of consciousness was through this quick discussion of Buddhist practices - at least it gave us an experimental basis for our claim.

As I have said before, this tradition based on the experience of people well practiced in the techniques of meditation, may not pass all the tests that scientists place on experimental results before they are accepted. One of them is repeatability: anyone with the right equipment should be able to obtain similar results. But here the equipment is the mind and its own mechanism for controlling its thoughts. And anybody who has tried to understand the behavior of people around them knows that these faculties are not equally developed in people. Moreover, very few people in the scientific community have taken meditation seriously, so we do not have a large sample of experiments and results. So my claim about the development of Karuna among practiced Buddhists is what scientists would call anecdotal.

Now the acceptability of an anecdote as a basis of serious study in science depends heavily on how foreign the result is. Just because someone observes something does not mean that someone else should repeat the experience. But how foreign the result is depends on the scientific theory and belief system. The very basis of Buddhist practice is outside the present pale of scientific discourse. So to bring it at least slightly closer to scientific acceptability I should make some effort to show some connection between our previous scientific hypothesis about the universal consciousness and the concept of Karuna. In what follows I propose to do that. As we move into that direction, we shall find that at least one more hypothesis would be needed about individual consciousness and some other related phenomena. Let us now get into that.

CHAPTER 6.
Morphogenesis and Complex Structures.

Our discussion starts from the description of a new form of memory similar to the one we discussed previously in relation to individual consciousness. However, it is not identical with it. The mechanism is different. This kind of memory seems to be operative in biological entities much larger than brain cells.

Let us start our discussion by considering how an embryo grows in the womb of the mother. The embryo starts as this single fertilized egg. But then it becomes a complete organism with various organs and functions in different parts of the body. And this happens just through repeated cell division. Modern molecular biology indicates that every cell has the same set of chromosomes in its nucleus. Yet each cell's structure is specific to its function, depending on the part of the body to which it belongs. The structure of all these organs is codified in the chromosomes in the cell. But how does the cell know which part of its chromosome should actually contribute to the structure of the organ? Biologists have suggested various models of how this may come about by the interaction of the genes with the proteins in the cell. The structure of these proteins, in their turn are influenced by the cells around them. Rupert Sheldrake[20] has discussed how our understanding of this process is far from clear. All the suggested mechanisms have pitfalls. He suggested an entirely different mechanism for informing the cells on how to develop. He suggested that this information comes, not just from the cell and its environment but from a so-called Morphogenetic Field. The picture is that the morphogenetic field of the organ carries the blueprint for its component cell structures. This field guides the morphogentic field of the cell, which carries the instruction for reading the genes in the cell – perhaps by the intermediary mechanism of the surrounding proteins.

Sheldrake's book on this topic, "A New Science of Life" was not received well by the community of Biologists. One journal called it "a book fit for burning". This is not because biologists had good explanations for the phenomena Sheldrake was trying to explain. It is just that his theory was outside materialism. So Biologists would not accept Sheldrake. They would rather pin their hopes on discovering the explanation in the future. It was not that Sheldrake had no credential as a biologist. He was well on his way to climbing the ladder of academic recognition at Cambridge and the Royal Society of London. But then he decided to break out into this new avenue of investigation. The reader will see similarities between this story and the story of Goswami. The reader will recall that Goswami challenged Physics regarding the reality of particles, since Physics can only predict the probability of their existence. His work also has been pointedly neglected.

It is not my purpose to expand on that theme of paradigm change here. However, I would like to remind the reader of the great tension between the Ptolemeic and the Copernican astronomy in the 1600's and the pressure brought to bear on Galileo. People like Goswami and Sheldrake are suggesting that science needs to change its long-standing "common sense" about materialism just as Copernicus challenged the common sense of Ptolemy and the church about geocentricity. Thus it is not surprising that people like Goswami and Sheldrake would face similar resistance. Only, society is much more genteel now, at least on the surface. So instead of the fear of inquisition and torture, such people do not have to face anything more than ridicule at worst and complete silence at best.

Let us get back to what Sheldrake was suggesting about Morphogenetic Fields and why.

Any time a complex structure (like a large crystal – even a large society) is built from smaller components the structure and behavior of the complex entity is impossible to predict from those of the component entities. "The whole is more than the sum of its parts" with properties of its own. Most of us know how the behavior of a crowd is very different from the behavior of most of its members. We shall discuss examples of a more "physical" nature presently.

When the assemblage is analyzed from the properties of the component parts, one often finds that the assemblage can take various different structures (predicted as configurations of minimum energy or other analogous scientific concepts). As to which of these structures the assemblage will take seems to be determined by its own independent laws, although the strict materialistic approach would claim that the structure and behavior of the organism can be predicted from the properties of the sub-atomic particles of which it is made. Perhaps it can be so predicted – but because of the size and complexity of the assemblage in comparison to that of the components, the calculations may take so long as to be beyond the scope of the fastest computers. That is why to this day Meteorology is not an exact science, even with the use of the fastest computers in the world. Moreover, even to get the calculation started one would have to know the configuration of each one of the components exactly – this in itself is impossible – for quantum theoretical reasons if for nothing else. Mathematics shows that except in systems of extreme simplicity ("linear systems") the state of the configuration is extremely sensitive to the initial states of the components. And the dependence of the configuration on the components shows very little pattern – a fact that has given this field of studies the popular name, "Chaos Theory". On the other hand, if the morphogenetic field is taken seriously and its properties studied carefully, one might get a much better handle on predicting the major aspects of morphgenesis – the growth of an organism from the fertilized cell.

There is one case where large assemblages have their property explicable in terms of the constituents - the study of gases. What we call pressure in a gas is accurately predictable as the average impact of the molecules of the gas, moving around almost at random and hitting the walls of the containing vehicle. So, the higher level property of pressure is predictable from the lower level property of the constituent molecules. However, we are talking about the average impact – not the individual impacts of each separate molecule, before they are averaged. Individual impacts would take impossibly long to calculate even if the initial configurations of the particles were known – and the initial configurations are not possible to know anyway.

Fortunately, we only need to know the average impact – the pressure. So one comfortably talks about the "gas laws" instead of the laws of particle motion. One is more or less confident that they know the connection between the two. So no one feels bad just talking about pressure rather than average impact. Studying how the way the pressure behaves in a gas suffices for all purposes. Studying the morphogenetic field instead of the exact materialistic mechanism of morphogenesis is a similar suggestion.

Laws of how the electrons, protons and neutrons come together to form atoms and how atoms come together to form smaller molecules can be analyzed with mathematical precision. However larger, more complex molecules like proteins – so essential to understanding morphogenesis - show behaviors which are hard to predict. Very fast computers take very long times to predict exactly how a protein molecule folds. Moreover, chaos theory predicts that even small changes in the constituent atoms would cause very large changes in the form of the molecule, just as we said above. The whole chain may get worked out for a small bacillus – we are close to getting there. But that will predict very little about the process in general - enough to get to an analog of pressure as we did above. We will have to be happy with an entirely different description.

That is why chemistry and biology are different subjects. So science begins to be somewhat useless in forming an uniform, continuous picture of the world. So, whether materialism can or can not form the basis of human knowledge and understanding is a moot point. And that is why it is important that the alternative approach – that of Morphogenetic Fields, is so important.

At this point it will be worthwhile to recall the way in which the collapse of the probabilities in the brain cell is influenced by the memory of the cell's previous collapse in response to observations. These observations come from the sensory organs, of course, so the morphogenetic field of the sense organs are now determining the memory, the morphogenetic field of the brain cells. We can even say that these observations by the senses carried out some purpose of the person whose senses and whose brain we are talking about. Just like the individual consciousness, the body has its morphogenetic field guiding the sensory organs. It is not only the eyes of a "dirty old man" that ogles young girls. The whole personality does.

Let us now try to understand how a body can influence the individual consciousness through the sensory stimuli. Let us recall that the forms of complex cell structures are dependent on the initial configurations of the elementary particles in it. The latter are subject to quantum uncertainity. Since the cell structures are observationally predictable (that is what biologists do), it looks like the way consciousness collapses these elementary particles into existence is guided more by the biological laws.

So it looks like there would be very little loss to the predictability in science if we said that matter behaves "as if" consciousness collapses elementary particles (and through them all other entities) under the guidance of these morphogenetic fields. That is, instead of thinking of large-scale phenomena arising out of the properties of small-scale phenomena, we can turn our views around and say that it is the requirements placed on the large scale phenomena that guide the properties of the small-scale phenomena. In the 1600's people started looking at the planetary motions "as if" they followed the Copernican model. As a result our understanding of the universe got improved. Similarly our study of Morphogenetic Fields will be more beneficial for understanding really large scale phenomena like humans and societies.

Now we have a second hypothesis in our extension to science – the hypothesis of "downward causation". That elementary particles comprising a complex structure are collapsed by consciousness in a way that fulfills the properties of the large scale structure.

What people like Sheldrake and Goswami would suggest is that we turn our point of view around this way. Instead of talking about how the atoms determine the molecules which in turn determine the cells which determine the organs which determines the organism, we say that the required form of the organism determines the required form of the organs which in turn determine the form of the cells and so on down to the atoms. So, the way consciousness collapses the elementary particles inside living things, is determined by the memories (the morphogenetic fields) of these higher entities.

One has to admit that only very small parts of this total picture presented here have been analyzed with scientific precision. It is as difficult a job as the development of our two-hundred-year old materialistic science has been. Such analysis would in no way refute the basic findings of materialistic science. Materialistic Science has been useful in the study of inert matter. But we need not use the strait-jacket of materialism in the analysis of complex thinking, acting organisms like living beings and societies. But such analysis suffers from a shortage of competent thinkers – the bias of materialism prevents people from trying this alternative paradigm of science.

The part of Sheldrake's thesis that drew the greatest amount of criticism from scientists was his explanation of how a morphogenetic field comes to be. The process he suggested, which he called "morphic resonance" is analogous to telepathy, a concept which is anathema to mainstream science. In our studies here, we introduce downward causation as an alternative hypothesis to morphic resonance[21]. As we have seen above, the morphogenetic field of any structure can be guided by the field of a larger structure containing it.

As we have said before, this picture can be extended upwards from organisms to societies, from objects to assemblages, from planets to milky ways to the entire creation. We shall see how this hypothesis of downward causation affects our thinking about spirituality and the society determined by such thinking. It will also have some influence on an alternative to "Social Darwinism" which leads away from the belief that selfishness is an important driving force towards the betterment of society.

CHAPTER 7.
Field to Soul to God – a flight of fancy.

The materialist says that the structure of life and society will eventually be understood by going from the components to the composite (reductionism – upwards causation). We are suggesting that we should study the way one can go from consciousness to complex structures down to simple structures till the existence of matter be understood. Scientific reductionism leads to greater complexity and to a harmful social order, especially under the influence of social Darwinism. Downward causation will simplify our understanding and lead to a more beneficial social order. In Chapter 5 we claimed that the Buddhist sages have found that meditation leads to Karuna, leading to a good social order. Now we shall try to explain how normal science, extended by the hypothesis of universal consciousness and downward causation can justify a more humane social order. Also this will counteract the arguments of the survival of the fittest. Let us see if this point of view makes some sense.

The materialist certainly can go on building more and more complex models. And though they do not quite understand life yet, they will agree that life occurs when a material structure reaches a certain level of complexity. They have not explained what a mind is either, but will agree that mind appears when there is a somewhat greater level of complexity. It seems that a mind capable of introspection occurs in extremely high orders of complexity among living objects. About consciousness the jury is out, but it seems more and more plausible that something called consciousness does not exist at all. In fact, say the materialist, consciousness is so difficult to define that debates about it may be quite futile.

Distinct from the materialist are the idealists. Idealists believe in the primacy of consciousness and the hypothesis of downward causation. The idealist agrees with almost all of the statements of the materialist about matter and its manifestations in the body and the brain. But they refuse to join the debate on consciousness. They do not agree that the building block of life and mind is matter. Their view is that the real source of all matter, including life, mind and body is consciousness. At the lowest level, the behavior of matter is known to be guided by quantum mechanics and some kind of a theory of higher organism can be built. But if that theory is based on materialism as its guiding "common sense", our efforts will be extremely difficult and may even be harmful.

Some may want to call this a religious view – although there are no trappings of institutionalized religion here: no alters, no incense, no dogma about a God, and certainly no need to vilify the espousers of "other" religions. Instead, we shall continue to call this view idealist or spiritual– for lack of any other technical term.

Let us pursue this idealist model of the world somewhat further. We shall try to build a model of the morphogenetic fields of structures of different complexity.

So far we have been looking at organisms, organs, cells and individual consciousness from the idealist point of view. Of these, only individual consciousness has found some support on the basis of quantum mechanics[22] and the hypothesis of the primality of universal consciousness. The rest of these structures are discussed on the basis of the incompleteness of the materialist view for going upwards from the simple to the complex. The materialist does not mind taking recourse to changing the hypothesis structure every time a certain threshold of complexity is crossed. It happens when molecular motion gives rise to gas pressure. It also happens when cells give rise to organs and then to organisms. Instead of these shifts of hypotheses we have suggested that we stop trying to explain everything from materialism and upward causation. Instead, we introduce the hypothesis of downward causation and the hypothesis of universal consciousness. These are used to build an uniform theory of the universe. Scientists are exhorted to direct their analysis and experiments to follow this alternate point of view. This may well lead to different techniques of observation and verification.

Let us now stop our effort at carefully maintaining a bridge to conventional science at every step. Let us indulge in an idealist flight of fancy. Let us imagine what might happen if we try to introduce consciousness at a level of highest complexity and build a hypothetical bridge towards quantum collapse by downward causation and consciousness.

We did make a passing reference to a crowd as an example of a structure made of organisms (humans in this case). But really we stopped with Sheldrake at the organism level. Our contact with existing science (conventional or extended) ends here and the fancy starts. We hope that scientific efforts of the future will point towards the feasibility of this view. But at the moment we shall make no effort to justify ourselves. We will just say that it will give some theoretical underpinning to one experimental fact: that deep meditation by practiced Buddhists leads to a compassionate view of the world.

So the first step up from organisms to societies is a first step upwards in complexity. Then comes the interaction of individuals and societies with the surrounding nature. From there we move from terrestrial nature to the planet earth in its totality. From there we advance to planetary systems to galaxies to the Universe. Perhaps there are other laterally related entities like black holes and double stars, but one can not be too precise in a flight of fancy.

At each level of this hierarchy, there is the related morphogenetic field which has its imprint on how the less complex entities below are structured and how they behave. And at the highest level of the structure we have the morphogenetic field of the universe as a whole. I personally would like to give it a name and indicate its special characteristics later. To do that we remind the reader that we have distinguished between organisms of different complexities. Organisms of lower complexities, whose structure is quite close to those dealt with by chemistry, we often call inanimate matter. Organisms of greater complexity show signs of life and biologists study those. At a higher level of complexity we say that these organisms have a mind that get studied by Psychologists. Sociologists study the structure of societies – of living organisms including organisms with minds. All of these studies have always claimed to have followed the materialistic, upward-causational model. We are suggesting that properties of societies do affect the behavior of the organisms in it. People are often creatures of their culture. Note that the same things are visualized differently in the western, middle-eastern and eastern cultures. So far they have remained distinct in spite of globalization. At another level it is being increasingly recognized that peoples' personalities often determine their physical health. "A-type" people are more prone to heart-attack, for instance. So the idea of downward causation is not far-fetched here.

We do not have much insight beyond this level of complexity. It may well be that practiced Buddhists have a level of complexity in their brains beyond other people. Even among the latter, some are more capable of self-analysis than others. Just to introduce our favorite nomenclature, we shall say that discerning organisms have something richer than a mind – they have a "self" and the more complex people have a "soul". And in our flight of fancy we shall posit that entities composed of organisms with a soul have souls also.

Let us call the soul of the universe, God. In Sanskrit, a word for this concept (i.e. what we are calling God) is "Viswatma": the soul of the universe. Let us follow this nomenclature.

At this point I shall ask my readers to divest themselves from many associations that have been formed with this word, "God". We are not visualizing that God created the earth, the sky, the camel, the hippopotamus, the microbe and mankind in the space of a week of October in 4004 BC. I am not suggesting that as Vishnu lay on the infinite ocean a lotus stock rose from His navel on which sat Brahma the creator who then proceeded to fashion heaven and earth. Let us not assume that God has set down rules which every human being is supposed to follow, that some specific groups of people have complete knowledge of what these rules are and have the responsibility and the right to enforce these rules on others. There are certainly some rules of nature – that of Physics, Chemistry and Biology and some which we may be in a position to discuss later. Breaking these rules may well have unpleasant consequences. Touching fire does burn one's hand. But let us not call these rules, "God's laws" yet. The only reason I am tempted to use this word "God" is that many people use this word – intentionally or unintentionally in a way which does not contradict our concept. Some of their views and practices (including those of the Buddhists and some (often villified) sects of Hindus, Christians, Jews and Muslims) can be discussed from an uniform point of view which is similar if not identical to the view here.

Let us remember that when we say "God" we are talking about a morphogenetic field. But it would not be wrong to realize that this is a very special morphogentic field. It is the morphogentic field of the most complex entity there is. So in our fancy let us realize that it is this field which guides the universe as well as everything in it, including humans with their minds and their souls – with their desires and their frustrations.

Let us recall the experimental fact that people who can meditate with success can rise above their desires and hence of their frustrations. As a matter of fact, it is not even necessary to talk about meditation. Let us talk about people who have had what psychologists call, "peak experiences".

In my experience and in the experience of those that I have talked to, during a peak experience one's frustrations seem irrelevant. All one's experience seem to be part of an unified whole. One person said, "It all makes sense". Many people's lives seem to get better organized after such experiences.

I shall assume following an analogy that God, in addition to having influence over and a closeness to all that exist is also close to universal consciousness. This closeness is greater than what people can feel during a peak experience or even during deep meditation. It is because of this closeness that God's purposes are guided by unity and compassion as it guides the universe and its components.

Having said all that one must still realize that the final agency in bringing about the structures guided by God are bound by the Quantum Mechanical probability laws. A collapse to an improbable state – leading to what we call a miracle – can occasionally occur, but phenomena which are impossible can not occur. Quoting an oft-quoted conundrum, "God can not make a stone so heavy he can not lift it." A miracle is not magic, designed to satisfy the desires in the neural structure of some individuals or groups.

But it also has to be understood that when a miracle happens, it happens as guided by "Karuna". We now have a motivation to talk about good and evil. We can take a Mother Teresa or a Albert Schweizer as miracles, but we have to take Adolf Hitler as a product of the neural conditioning of a warped individual consciousness.

Such a world view removes the last materialist argument for selfish destruction of society – "survival of the fittest". Let us now move on to that.

CHAPTER 8.

Evolution to the materialist and the idealist.

The theory of evolution develops an explanation of how the present life forms came to be. It must explain not only the forms around our immediate vicinity, but also others. It must explain those found in far reaches of the world where some unusual forms are present. It must not only explain the foxes and dogs in Europe and Asia but must also explain the Kangaroo and the Koala bear in Australia. It must also explain those extinct species whose evidence we find in fossils.

Darwin developed a large part of his theory while traveling around the world observing various species of fauna and flora. Simulteneously with his work Gregor Mendel[23] (a monk who made an extensive study of hybrid peas raised by himself in the monastery gardens). was discovering the laws of genetics. Darwin had to build his theory with due attention to these other theories and his own observations. Darwin and his followers also had to bring that theory in line with fossil findings.

It will be noticed that this model of theory formation followed the accepted scientific lines. Newtonian mechanics did not just explain how the apple fell on Newton's head. It also explained and predicted how the planets and satellites move in the sky, how a snowball gathers speed and many other cases of motion. Darwinian theory also explained not only the existent species, like humans, but also their relationship to similar species like apes and Lemurs. A large part of biological and geological observations were well explained by the Darwinian theory of evolution. But there are some uncomfortable problems with it also just as there is with materialist quantum mechanics. And here we shall indicate how the extensions suggested by us may be of help.

So we aim to follow the same path as we trod in our discussion of Physics and its needed extension. In the case of our discussion of Physics we first described the expected view in physics. Then we proceeded to discuss what was unsatisfactory about it. After that we introduced a necessary modification. Let us now proceed to do that for the Darwinian theory of evolution.

We shall skip the origin of life and living species. The origin of life is still not well understood in science. Darwinian theory does encompass the very primitive forms of life as well as later developments. For a simplified discussion of that let us start with the assumption that we have a set of species already established and theorize about what happens to them as time passes.

The species replicate over generations following the laws of genetics, whose bio-chemical basis is understood by now. The structure and behavior of DNA molecules have been studied and are being studied. It has already been pointed out above that the relation between the genes in the cells and the development of embryos need downward causation for a satisfactory explanation. Leaving that behind, let us look at the reasons why species change and also how new species develop.

Genetics itself tells us that there will be variations inside a species. Some people are tall and lean, some are short and chubby. Some have blue eyes, some have brown eyes. Now in general, it may happen that some of these types have a slight edge over other types with respect to their ability to grow healthy and replicate – some may die before reproductive age. Some races of humans are more and less prone to some kinds of diseases than others. But these do not stand in the way of perpetuation of the human race. But in the past these differences may have been crucial among some species, including some of our ancestor species. This leads to one kind of mechanism by which some variants of one specie may grow more rapidly than other variants – leading to a slow change in the characteristics of species.

How do these and more pronounced variations come to be? They visualize that from time to time, under radioactive bombardment from cosmic rays and other causes, some genes change their structure by small amounts. These give rise to a slightly different specie and these changes are genetically transmitted through generations. If this changed species are more suited to their environment they will become more numerous than the original species. The original species may die out in competition with the new species. Or they may continue if major competition is not involved. This coexistence may well be the reason why some people are tall and lean and others short and chubby.

So this idea of random change and natural selection of the fit species ("survival of the fittest") is the major driving force behind evolution according to the Darwinian theory. And as I have said, it explains quite a bit of the biological and geological data. But there is a major phenomenon that seems to be left out by this theory. We are talking about the emergence of totally different species. We may also talk about the emergence of a much improved organ in an existing specie. These do not come to be by gradual change from old species. Often there is no geological evidence of these gradual changes. Also, genetic theory does not support any mechanism for such large changes.

Let us look at these two discrepancies. First, note that geological or fossil evidence do show the gradual changes in species as predicted by Darwinian theory. Major changes do occur in a specie - enough to call it the emergence of a new specie. However, one finds no evidence in the fossils for the gradual change leading to these new species. In the smooth flow of small improvements in a specie a new specie suddenly appears. This phenomenon is called "punctuated equilibrium" in geological literature. It has been studied and analyzed by the late Stephen Jay Gould[24], Fellow of the National Institute of Science and his collaborators.

But this discrepancy with Darwinian theory really is what we would expect, since it appears in a different form in the bio-chemistry of the cells in the new species. A new specie differs from an old specie in many genetic aspects – it is not that just one gene is changed; many genes change at the same time. If only the small component changes occurred at any time, the resulting changed specie would not make it better suited to the environment: it would probably die out very quickly. For these new improved specie to develop, a simultaneous change of many genes would be needed. Now recall that genes change by random cosmic events. The chance of the change of any one gene is small. So the chance of simultaneous change of many genes is small indeed. So the evolution of new species would be much slower than what the geological evidence shows. What is going on here?

Materialist Science has been wrestling with this problem in evolution in various ways. We shall introduce at this point our way of explaining this from downward causation – originating probably at God. Of course, our thoughts in this line is not so well developed that we can rule out its origin at a lower level of complexity. It can not be explained just by the collapse of cells by universal consciousness. Our theory will have to ascribe some kind of purpose in the higher morphogenetic fields – but since we have not claimed any duality in the universal consciousness, no purpose can be ascribed to it.

I have referred to the work of Dawkins in explaining non-selfish behavior among humans on the basis of survival of the fittest. That work is cogent and may well be related to what we are discussing here. But instead of trying to find that relation, let us continue with the idealist view here.

Our view is that the simultaneous change of genes is indeed an event of low probability as predicted by Quantum Mechanics and the "undesirable" changes of single genes in the set are indeed more probable. But the low probability event is the one which is collapsed to reality in the interest of creating an improved form of life. The undesirable but more probable events either do not occur or lead to a very unfit specie. But the low probability event occurs much more frequently than is predicted by probabilities.

Such a picture does presuppose a purposefulness in the laws of science – and the only way we can explain such a purpose is by invoking downward causation. Some biologists outside the mainstream call this picture as coming out of a "design theory".

Unfortunately this has led some fundamentalist Christian organizations to demand that design theory be taught in high school. But as far as mainstream biology is concerned this is a theory under development. All ongoing research is not fit for introducing into secondary curricula. In this I am in agreement with mainstream science. I do not visualize teaching relativity theory in secondary curricula either except in very accelerated courses (I personally have not been able to explain the Einstein-Minkowski model of the space-time continuum so far to my very bright grandson in high school). Moreover, the mainstream scientists are opposed to the proposal of the fundamentalists that design theory be taught in high school. They have a suspicion that this is just the first step before demanding that we teach about the creation of all existing species on an October day in 2004 BC. The matter has become a political rather than a scientific discussion. I am therefore staying out of this discussion. I shall await a time when a saner discussion of the hypotheses of universal consciousness and downward causation emerges as an integrated extension to science. I have a sneaking suspicion that such a discussion will not be to the liking of the fundamentalists.

But one may raise the question of why the purpose behind evolution is a necessary consequence of Karuna. This may perhaps require a new axiom. However, in our flight of fancy we may look at it as follows.

As we know, the existence of an individual consciousness is a prerequisite for an observation to occur. If nothing existed except for the eternal universal consciousness, the world as we know it would not be there. There would not be a God either. Let us take it as an extra hypothesis that God needs to exist. So the need to create is an extra property that we can ascribe to universal consciousness. At the same time, the very nature of creation entails a separation of the individual and universal consciousness. And this alienation is the source, not only of observation, but also of desires and frustrations and sorrow - even in God. So there is this opposite tendency for conscious beings to remove the alienation. It is this process which leads to the desire in conscious beings to realize the universal consciousness in their own selves. This is the goal of Buddhist meditation, and some form of meditation is recommended by the mystics in every religion.

For meditation to occur, a created entity must not only be alive and conscious. It must also have enough power of retrospection to understand the phenomenon of alienation. That is the main difference between machines and humans. So this phenomenon of creation and evolution of conscious introspective beings is an integral part of this tension between creation and non-existence. Hindu cosmology looks at the universal phenomenon as an oscillation arising out of this tension between the need to exist and the need to remove alienation. Hence during the part of the cycle where primordial life develops into introspective beings, while creation is still at work, God (as here defined) would guide evolution towards the development of species capable of introspection.

CHAPTER 9.
From Flights of Fancy to Established Practices.

In previous chapters we have argued that the concepts of universal and individual consciousness can be considered to be extensions of Science as presently understood. Compared to that, the idea of God and of His guidance in evolution were based on much more tenuous grounds. Some object to these latter concepts and the flights of fancy that gave rise to these. But to our mind there is still value in pursuing further into the idea of consciousness and possible experimental verifications of the associated theory.

There is a so-called "scientific" objection to the consciousness–centered view-point from the conventional scientists. They say that there is experimental evidence about the laws of matter discovered by science, but there is no such evidence for the spirit. They are right only in the first half of this sentence. Scientific experiments have been directed to understanding matter and the experiments were designed with that purpose. Methods for experimentation regarding the spirit need entirely different methods of observation and analysis. Most vocal material scientists have not been acquainted with them or accepted them. The methods of experimentation on the spirit are subjective, and science has eschewed subjectivity so far. Of course, there were very good reasons for avoiding subjectivity. However, it is our belief that there is need for the development of methodologies which will be able to test the validity of experiments on subjective phenomena. Some workers in parapsychology[25] have taken tentative steps in this direction. For the present, however, it may be well to recognize one thing. People who have attempted such subjective experiments are personally convinced of their validity and people who observe them have reason to believe in their validity. We have already referred to Buddhist practices in this connection. This may be a good place to discuss the matter further.

It needs to be pointed out that the Buddhists are not the only group of people who have taken the idea of meditation seriously. Hindu philosophers who discuss universal consciousness have developed a theory of consciousness and an experimental method for verifying it. This theory and these methods are the central part of the Vedantic school of Hindu religion. The methods are very similar to the Buddhist methods. A very good source of the description of these latter practices can be found in a book by Prof. Charles Tart[26]. We are emphasizing his book over many others because it is written by a well-known psychologist. Dr. Tart has made a name for himself in the study of consciousness. What we discuss below is closely related to the techniques described by him. Many authors described these methods in many places in the world over a long period of time. The fact that these are not taken seriously by conventional scientists does not necessarily detract from the seriousness of what these people have described and experienced.

Apart from the kind of disciplined experimentation described by these various people, there have been subjective experiences by people of scientific credibility which have also been studied. We have already referred to "peak experiences". Often scientists do not want to own up to having had such experiences for fear of ridicule by their peers and possible loss of recognition in their field. Charles Tart has been compiling a listing of personal experiences of scientists[27] (including scientists in the physical sciences). These people have established credentials. Tart has encouraged these reporters by assuring them that their identities will only be known to him – their stories appear over pseudonyms if the authors so desire. This is a piece of side information for the curious reader. For our purposes we shall stick to descriptions of directed, consciously pursued experiments.

The practice of meditation is not limited to followers of Hinduism and Buddhism alone. Mystics in most religious traditions have described methods of meditation. Among Muslims, there are the Sufis. To the best of my belief and knowledge, these traditions are accepted in Judaism and various Christian Churches including the Roman Church. To the extent that a theoretical basis for these practices occur in these traditions, they may well be different from the basis accepted by the Hindus. The Hindu theory is similar to the one espoused by us on Quantum Mechanical grounds.

Among Muslims and Christians, as well as among some Hindu and Buddhist sects, the theory involving consciousness are not given central place. The one Christian sect which takes meditation seriously are the Quakers. My knowledge and understanding are limited to the theories and practices of the Buddhists, Vedantic Hindus and Quakers. I shall discuss these in a religion-independent manner.

One upshot of this discussion will be that the Quakers method of what they call "Worship" can very well be conducted in ways leading to understanding ("observing?") the universal consciousness. It needs to be noted that their methods are not in contradiction to the Eastern methods. The basis of the Eastern methods have been used and tested by many people – famous and not-so-famous – for about four thousand years. So our discussion has to go somewhat further back in time to when the Vedntic and the Buddhist practices took shape.

The Vedantic method of meditation is called Jnana-Yoga – union with the universal consciousness through meditation and study. It dictates that we need to remove the obstruction in the way of our salvation i.e. our feeling of unity with the universal consciousness. This obstruction is identified with the ego - our desires in all their form, from value judgments to compulsions. These form the integral part of what we have called the individual consciousness in previous sections. On the other hand, the followers of the Sankhya duality, instead of dwelling on the distinction between God ("Ishwara") and the universal consciousness (the "Paramatma"), take the adoration of Ishwara as the supreme method to salvation. Here also the ultimate in adoration and worship is the complete surrender of the self to God. This in its turn leads to the removal of the same obstructions. This is the Eastern method of "Bhakti-yoga" (union through adoration). In either form, the feeling of union with the whole world leads to compassion for the pains of others. As long as one is aware of one's own pain and needs to remove the source of that pain, one can not neglect the pain in others and the need to remove that pain. This leads to activism in the devout, led by the concept of "Seva" (service). However, this service also is a result of the union, not a striving for "righting all wrongs". The latter attaches a desire (a "purpose") to the action. The Yoga of action ("Karma Yoga") dictates that the action should not be contaminated with any desire for the result.

So the Hindus subscribe to different ways of understanding consciousness. Which path one chooses depends on one's natural propensities – the form of their individual selves. There is the path of meditation and study, the path of pure adoration, the path of action in the performance in one's service to society.

Buddhists of the Teravada school emphasize meditation, but they prefer to make meditation a purely experimental process without going into a theoretical discussion like the Hindus (or like the kind of Scientists that I would like to see).

Quakers follow paths of meditation, adoration and service as a total path. Naturally however, different Quaker practitioners emphasize these different paths according to their preference.

All these schools of thought would probably agree that they are following religious practices. I shall however, continue to resist the use of the term "religion". In all parts of the world, that word has been misused to a great extent and have given rise to various social ills. Let us call them different spiritual methods.

All of these methods are similar, as I have said before. Let me look at these methods in their similarity and occasional slight differences.

Quakers, Hindus and Buddhists suggest that the practitioners develop a certain set of attitudes towards life. The Quakers codify these in what they call "testimonies" and "advices". It is not clear to me whether Quakers consider these to be an integral part of their meditational life or just as a part of a general good life. Hindus have practices associated towards the development of these attitudes. Both Hindus and Buddhists have different names for the different aspects of the attitudes – we need not go into them here. But they do consider these to be an integral part of the spiritual practice. I shall go on my personal belief (based partly on experience) that these attitudes help in the meditational process. The meditation in its turn strengthens these attitudes. In the next few paragraphs I shall try to describe and summarize these attitudes and the connection between them and the individual self.

(1) One needs to come to the realization that one is an extremely small part of the universe. Similarly one's life is of infinitesimal length compared to that of the entire creation. Thus, the self is not a terribly important thing worth a huge amount of attention and pampering. Such an attitude may lead to a withdrawal from the surroundings. Hindus and Budddhists do allow such withdrawal. However unless one is very careful, such withdrawal may well become pathological. On the other hand, this same realization may lead to an attitude of "eat,

drink and be merry for tomorrow ye die". This attitude is not conducive to good mental health or a constructive life either.

Most people would find the contemplation of such approaches unsatisfactory. One could however, develop some goals in life which are not tied up with one's selfish desires. The goals may be spiritual, social, scientific or other non-personal purposes. One risk associated with the pursuit of such goals is that one might associate the successes and failures of the goals with one's own personal successes or failures. Such association defeats the purpose of such goals, since it brings oneself into the center of attention again. One has to look upon the pursuit of the goal as merely the expression of the fact that one exists and the goal exists also; this minimizes the risk of extreme attachment.

(2) One needs to develop compassion and understanding towards other people and other living objects. Their faults and weaknesses, as well as their troubles and sorrows are not too different from our own faults, weaknesses, troubles and sorrows. This attitude reduces the risk of undue expectations, angers and disappointments. It also reduces the tendency to self-importance.

(3) One has to learn to evaluate all desires as conducive, non-conducive and obstructive to one's overall goal. All goals can be pursued better if one's attitudes towards all desires and needs are balanced ones. One can also develop the ability to ask if one

desire is getting in the way of another. The desire for a sports car can get in the way of the desire for a balanced budget. The desire for a balanced budget should not get in the way for the desire for a medicine required for one's physical well-being.

All this is common sense, of course, but this practice can be difficult unless one makes this in conjunction of all the disciplines given here and the practice of meditation itself. Continuing with that one must also

(4) develop the habit of keeping control over reflex behaviors like anger, greed and other propensities which can get in the way of a balanced view of life.

None of these above attitudes are easy to achieve. As any experimental scientist knows, no disciplined experiment is easy to pursue. One may well expect to deviate from them at one time or another. One should guard against making such failures the occasion for self-loathing, disappointment or despondence. All these are again occasions for attaching too much importance to ones own self, as we discussed in connection with attitude 1 above. Efforts fail just because they fail – they may well be considered as important as successes. They are just phenomena. The idea is to develop as dispassionate a view of life as possible.

The best news is that all these disciplines become easier to follow if practiced diligently and in concomitance with the practice of meditation. This latter we now proceed to describe[28].

Before this time I have referred to meditation as an experiment. The main instrument in this experiment is one's own mind. So, just as in any scientific experiment, one has to make sure that the instrument is as suited as possible to the experiment. The development of the attitudes described above can be taken to be conducive to the improvement of the mind as an instrument for the experiment.

Going on to the experiment itself, it is not a one-time experiment as many experiments in materialist science are. There are experiments in Chemistry and Biology that take an extended period of time to complete. The completion of a reaction or the germination and growth of a plant can take a long time. The meditational experiment also needs to be continued over a very long period of time – perhaps stretching over years. It has to be performed on a regular schedule. The Hindus and the Buddhists recommend a daily practice, one or more times a day at regular times. Quakers do not have clear instructions on daily meditation. They attach greater emphasis on a regular, at least once-a-week practice. While Hindus and Buddhists seem to take it for granted that the daily meditation can well be performed alone, the Quakers attach great importance to conducting the practice in a group. They probably rely on the influence of a social morphogenetic field to make the experiment more effective. This group activity is commonly called "worship", although any comparison with other practices would show very little difference between a Hindu meditation and a Quaker worship.

The period of time for which the meditation is to be performed is fixed to a great extent by social decree in the case of Quakers. They meditate anywhere from 45 minutes in some local groups (called, "meetings") to hours in some. When it comes to individual meditation, it is my opinion that the time should depend on the ability of the practitioner. Trying to force oneself to a long period of practice seems to be useless. People in a group worship can testify to the fact that not all worshippers can hold their attention on the experiment for the same length of time.

The actual practice of meditation consists in holding one's attention steadily on one single thing – desirably for the entire period of practice. This thing could be anything, so far as I know: a pebble or a button will do. People associated with a specific religious tradition concentrate on some icon. Some Buddhists use an intricate geometric pattern (a "Mandala"). In Buddhist "Mindfulness Meditation" the concentration is on the process of breathing in the initial phases. Hindus often use the picture of a deity. Christians are encouraged to concentrate on the figure of Christ, perhaps on the cross. Atheists, naturally have no alternative than to concentrate on some material object. The most austere, Vedantic school of Hindus urge one to concentrate on a total state of non-existence: they use the analogy of the experience of deep, dreamless sleep. Quakers use the word, "silence", perhaps to signify the same state, or perhaps to the state of freedom from thoughts: they do not have specific instructions. They believe that everyone's method has to be engineered along the individuals state of spiritual growth. In this they are probably correct. It is my personal belief as a Quaker that while there are indeed individual differences, there needs to be some picture of a common ideal. Perhaps the word "silence" is all that the Quakers feel comfortable with in sketching out this ideal. I have heard good Vedantists use the same word.

Within a short time of starting the practice, it becomes obvious that an extended holding of attention on a single thing is very hard to do. Thoughts of various nature interfere constantly with the concentration, grabbing attention away. This tendency needs to be controlled, of course. But this control should never be exercised with great mental violence or anger. One just gently nudges the mind back to the object of concentration. In the process, one gets some insights into what is and is not important to one's individual psyche. If one feels like pondering on them, such pondering should not interfere with the practice itself. It should be put off as something to be done at some other time. Else the mind gets distracted from the concentration into channels of self-analysis.

What has gone above is just a generalized summary of the only kind of experiment that is well developed among people who take spirituality seriously. People who claim to follow a "religion" may have other recommended practices and such practices may or may not be good adjuncts to what we have written here. But this is not a good place to discuss these. I am also desisting from giving major details about the practice as followed by different schools. The interested readers will have to find their own references for these – anything I give will be bound to be incomplete.

As I have been saying all along, I consider these practices as valid scientific experimentation. Materialistic scientists may well feel that these practices lack the non-subjective approach which is essential in all materialist experimentation. However, given the nature of the theory these are supposed to verify, this is inevitable. However, there may be one saving grace for the materialistic purist. Scientists who have tried to study the encephalograms of people in meditation have found a distinct change in the brain waves of the meditator as time progresses. These changes do have a subjective correlate – the meditator does report that their concentration on the silence does deepen as time progresses. The brain waves return to normal as people come out of their deep concentration. So the subjective perception does have some correlate in material observations.

CHAPTER 10.
Concluding Summary.

I have written this book with the purpose of proposing an effective method for pulling society back from the self-destructive path which it is following. I do not know if everybody will agree with me that the root of this problem is very deep. Many people believe that changing this or that social policy is all that is needed, and many efforts are made towards such ends. My own belief is that the problem is rooted in our materialistic belief system itself. Many fundamentalist religious movements state that the cure for this would be the espousing of this or that religious dogma. I believe that these also are extremely harmful. One needs a system of belief which can not be easily bent into the concentration of power in the hands of the few. One needs a belief system where the very idea of individual power becomes socially unacceptable. It does not matter whether this power is wielded by the religious, political, economic or intellectual leadership. One needs a system where power is ascribed to something outside the human condition.

One such promising system is the one espoused by the scientists – that the source of all truth is experimentation. The laws one discovers about the nature of things are independent of human manipulation. This could indeed be a viable point of view – except for two things. It does not lead to a basis of compassion in society and balance in the ecology, as I have discussed before. Also, science unfettered by a social value system leads to a concentration of power into the hands of the technological elite. The discovery of any technology, no matter how socially valuable, gets warped into a device for profit. This vitiates from the full social benefit of the discovery. Also, harmful innovations like weapons of destruction also gets developed to enhance the centralization of power further.

One may well expect that strong religious beliefs would lead away from such harmful effects. But historically this has never happened. Religion has merely yielded further weapons of mass control.

Pure science, with its message of impersonality, is a desirable approach. But it needs to be coupled with a theoretical base which lead to the classical values of compassion and balance. What I am trying to do is to provide such a base. It in no way takes away from the validity of science, giving man the same power over matter that it has been giving. However, it adds a "why" to the "how" of science. And I am claiming that, far from restricting science, it will open science out into further avenues of useful inquiry into the nature of the world.

APPENDIX.
The nature of logical thinking and its limitation.

To the logician, a theory is merely a collection of sentences. A subset of the sentences in the theory is designated as the set of axioms. The rest of the sentences in the theory follow from the axioms by logical deduction. A theory is acceptable to a logician as long as it does not contain two sentences which are negations of each other. A theory, to be acceptable, has merely to be consistent.

A scientific theory has to have more structure. In addition to the axioms (which are often designated as laws or hypotheses), there are some sentences which are derived from observations. There are criteria in science as to when an observation can be accepted as reliable. In a scientific theory all the reliable observations are required to be derivable from the axioms.

It was shown in the mid-thirties by the mathematician Kurt Goedel that logical quantitative theories are limited. Now science has been most successful with quantification of observation. So they, by their very nature, set limitations to their power. The exact symbolic and technical nature of those difficulties can not be discussed in the available space here[29]. So we shall ask the readers to accept as true the following three facts about the language of the symbolic logic of quantitative science:

1. There is a method of symbolic representation available in which one can express laws of science. The method is not dependent on what the laws are. However, it has been sufficient to express all the laws we have needed to express so far. There is also a symbolic method available for deducing all consequences of given laws from a statement of the laws. This method is what the study of formal or informal logic is all about and includes the methods of normal mathematics.

2. It has been proven that given a set of laws, the rules of deduction can deduce all the facts that are true in every world governed by these laws. They also can disprove all facts that cannot hold in a world governed by these laws.

3. Also proven is that, given any set of laws, one can always write down sentences which can neither be proved nor disproved on the basis

of these laws. For our future discussion we shall call these sentences "undecidable from these laws".

These three facts, when taken together say something quite disturbing about our ability to describe the world by means of scientific laws. Any undecidable sentence as described above is still the expression of a fact. So this fact either holds for our world or it does not. Suppose it holds. Since it cannot be proved, and since anything which is true in a world described by the laws is provable from the laws (see 2 above), clearly the laws have not described the world sufficiently well.

Similarly if the fact does not hold in our world, then we should be able to disprove it, but we can not do that either so the laws we have formulated for this world do not even tell us that this fact is untrue in the world. So the only way we can establish this fact or refute it in our world would have to be determined by some experiment or other. Our laws of the world would then have to be modified to take into account the results of that experiment.

Something of this nature happened in the last century and by an accident of history became a part of our scientific heritage. Euclid can be credited with laying the foundation of the logical or "axiomatic" method in mathematics. He expressed the geometrical properties of space by using what we would call the modern logical (or axiomatic) method. In his

"Elements" he put down as "obvious" certain facts about points, lines, angles, etc. For example, he took it as an axiom that through two distinct points exactly one straight line can be drawn. From this and some other initial axioms he could deduce many facts about geometrical figures (for example, "the sum of the three angles of any triangle is equal to the sum of two right angles"). Now one of his axioms (about parallel lines) did not seem very obvious to later geometers, and they wondered if it really could be proven from the other axioms. All these efforts failed and finally a number of mathematicians suggested that since the negation of this axiom does not seem to contradict the other axioms, perhaps it would be consistent to assume that this axiom does not have to hold. Other axioms were used to replace it and different geometries were obtained. It was found that while the geometry with Euclid's postulate held for planes, other postulates held for other surfaces, like spheres and saddles.

It was also seen that small parts of these other surfaces deviated from Euclid's axiom by only very small amounts, so his geometry could continue to be used on our very large (albeit spherical) earth. However, it was not until Einstein's theory of relativity suggested that space close to a massive object is curved that one could perform an experiment to establish as to which postulate held in the real world. It was found that our space, instead of following the postulate of Euclid, follows the postulate for a curved space.

Unfortunately that does not tell us everything about our world either. Rule 3 above says that even with this new set of laws we would again be faced with a sentence which can neither be proved nor disproved. Now since this specific question may not be answered with a "yes" or a "no", we can include the "yes" answer as an axiom in our logic and work with that as our new science. But then we could also have appended the "no" answer to our logic as an axiom, giving rise to a different science. Both of these sciences would be consistent as logical theories. Which science would one choose? Either perform an experiment to decide or choose the one which agrees with the conventional wisdom of the time. But if we do the latter, how do we know that the resulting science is correct? That was the problem which gave rise to the schism between the church and Copernicans, as we have seen before. Also, if some experiment does decide between the two sciences, that logical system would give rise to another unanswerable question. So if we insist on being logical, one would forever be adding new axioms to science. Of course, this would keep on enriching science. And this is true whether we decide to live with the logical problem with Universal and Individual consciousness or not. It may even be necessary to drop logic at some point. How long we wait before we do that is really more a matter of taste and social needs.

Thus there may not be any way for us to describe the world by means of scientific laws: something would always remain beyond the reach of scientific laws. So if the scientific method as it is now known is the only instrument available to us for knowing the truth, then we are forever doomed to have an incomplete science.

On the basis of the above discussion it can be cogently argued that while logical theories and experimentation can be used to refine science to any degree we please, a precise and complete theory of the nature of the world can not possibly be logical. The relation between the new science and the logical theory we have today can perhaps be compared to the relation between real numbers and fractions.

Recall, for instance, that while the square root of two can be expressed by fractions to any specified degree of precision, the exact square root of two is from a different class of numbers distinct from the fractions. Mathematicians use very different techniques for studying numbers like the square root of two. In the same way we cannot carry out a debate on the limitations of materialism by using the logical method, especially since the logical method can always be used to approach the true nature of the world to any refinement needed. This might place our extended science as beyond knowledge – as long as we claim that language can be the only repository of knowledge. Language-limited knowledge can take us as close to truth as needed for any specific purpose. But to go beyond the paradoxes of such knowledge (as arises in our discussion that observations need the identity of the part and the whole) we need different modes of acquiring knowledge. Such knowledge, if acquired or if accepted can be used in discussions, but such discussion always carries the risk one runs anytime one uses undefined terms.

ENDNOTES

1   Lerner, M.,"The politics of meaning", New York, Addison Wesley (1996)

2   Dawkins, R., *The Selfish Gene*, Oxford, The Oxford University Press (1990)

3   New York, Perennial Library (1973)

4   Boulding, K., *Beyond Economics: Essays on Society, Religion and Ethics*, Ann Arbor, U. of Michigan Press (1968)

5   Dennett, D., Consciousness Explained, Boston, Little, Brown and Co. (1991)

6   Kurzweil, R., Age of Spiritual Machines, *Sagebrush Educational Resources* (2000)

7   New York, Simon and Schuster (1985)

8   Roberts and Co. (2003)

9   (Lettvin et al, "What the Frog's Eye tells the Frog's Brain", Proc. I.R.E., Vol 47, 1959)

10 Science Desk, April 13 2004.

11 The Man Who Mistook His Wife for a Hat, Picador, London, 1985

12 *Ibid*

13 Kuhn, Thomas S., *The structure of Scientific Revolutions*, University of Chicago Press (1962).

14 *ibid*

15 Gamow, G., The New World of Mr. Tompkins, Cambridge, Cambridge University Press (2001).

16 Erwin Schroedinger, one of the pioneers of Quantum Mechanics brought this conundrum to the notice of scientists in 1935 in the journal *Naturwissenschaften*.

17 Goswami, A., *The Self-Aware Universe: How Consciousness Creates the Material World,* New York, Putnam/Tarcher, (1993).

18 Dennett, D., Consciousness Explained, Boston, Little, Brown and Co. (1991)

19 Mitchell, M and Goswami, A, "Quantum Mechanics for Observer Systems", *Physics Essays,* 5 (1992), pp. 526-529.

20 Sheldrake, R., *A New Science of Life*, Los Angeles, Tarcher (1981).

21 I need to add that our avoidance of morphic resonance is because of the need of axiomatic simplicity only. We disagree with the mainstream scientist's revulsion against telepathy. But any discussion of this disagreement is not relevant to our present discussion.

22 Mitchell and Goswami, *ibid.*

23 Mendel's detailed paper, "Versuche Uber Pflanz-Hybride" was presented at a meeting of the Zoologist Botanischer of Vienna in 1865.

24 Gould. S., *Ever Since Darwin; Reflections on Natural History,*W.W.Norton (1992)

25 Radin, D., *The Conscious Universe*, San Francisco, HarperEdge (1997)

26 Tart, C., *Mind Science; Meditation Training for Practical People,*Novato, CA, Wisdom Editions (2001)

27 See the web site http://www.issc-taste.org/index.shtml

28 In addition to Tart (*ibid*) see also Prabhavananda and Isherwood, C., *How to Know God: The Yoga Aphorisms of Patanjali,* Hollywood, Vedanta Press (1953).

29 A very readable discussion of these details appear in Hofstadter, D. R, *Goedel, Escher, Bach: An Eternal Golden Braid*, New York, Basic Books (1979) in Chapters 7,8 and 9. Instead of calling the subject "symbolic logic of quantitative science" he has called it TNT (Typographical Number Theory – carrying with it a hint of an explosion) in his characteristic tongue-in-cheek style.

ABOUT THE AUTHOR

Dr. Banerji received his doctorate in Physics from Calcutta University, India, in 1956. He joined the Case Institute of Technology as an assistant Professor in 1961 and was promoted to Professor in 1968. He moved to the east coast in 1973 and retired from Saint Joseph's University in Philadelphia as Professor of Mathematics and Computer Science in 1992.

Dr. Banerji has authored two books and edited three others, in the field of Computer Science. He is a Fellow of the American Association for Artificial Intelligence. He has published about ninety technical papers on Ionospheric Physics and various branches of Computer Science.

As invited Visiting Professor Dr. Banerji has taught at the University of Paris, Calcutta University, the University of Vienna, the Vienna Technical University and the Technical University of Prague.

Since his retirement one of his major interests has been the connection between science and the basis of various religions.

Printed in the United States
54354LVS00001B/21

9 781425 931124